HOW TO ESCAPE FROM
PRISON

HOW TO ESCAPE FROM
PRISON

EMOTIONAL FREEDOM
DOESN'T JUST HAPPEN -
IT'S CLAIMED.
HERE'S HOW.

DEVAN BAILEY

FOUNDER OF SHAPING REALITY

For information contact:
Shaping Reality
525 Route 73 North STE 104,
Marlton, NJ 08053

https://www.shapingreality.com

ISBN **978-1-7340259-0-3**

First published September 2019

To my wife: Nicola. Thank you for standing beside me through this transformation. I know it isn't easy. The faith and trust you place in me is quite remarkable. You are the person I most want to be proud of me.

Table of Contents

A Letter From Me to You

I'm sure, like me, you've had deep and meaningful thoughts about why you're here and what you're *supposed* to be doing. Personally, I've always had a feeling inside that I was supposed to be doing something "bigger". I always thought on some level that I was living a lie and not doing what I was destined to do. But I never had the courage or the clarity to act on these feelings and explore other avenues. I believed that the rat race was the only option for me, so I just accepted things as they were and only dreamt of more.

I had a daily routine (I'm sure you've experienced this too): waking up to your alarm, dreaming for a split second there's been a mistake and it's actually the weekend, and longing to go back to sleep!

I feel your pain. Life at the office is really hard. The constant stress, pressure and expectations at work really get to us. You feel like you're moving from one crisis to the next. You're always rushing around and feeling short on time. It feels like nothing you do is good enough and you live in constant fear of letting someone down.

We never process these feelings – we just live with the anxiety and worry that comes with the job. We put it down to "life" and accept what happens as "outside of our control", as though somehow these painful, often unbearable, experiences are a badge of honor; part of climbing the corporate ladder.

Is this really all there is to life?

No. It doesn't have to be this way. It really doesn't!

I used to call my office a "glamorous prison". It was a terrible and disempowering way to view my situation, but this is easy to do when you genuinely feel imprisoned and can't see a way out. But, here's the thing: when you're in a tough job, you're not really "locked up". That is your perception keeping you trapped in an emotional prison – a prison created by you; your mind.

This book is going to show you how to escape that prison. You'll learn that, in fact, you have at your disposal the tools needed to break free *right now*. You'll learn the **ten** simple tools to make it happen. You'll also learn how to access those tools and use them to take huge steps towards finding happiness and fulfillment, irrespective of your current circumstances. You'll discover how to break free from the mental and emotional prison in which you find yourself incarcerated.

Emotional freedom is not about your company, your job, your career, or the people you work with. It's about you. It's about your mindset, your programming, your perception, and your beliefs. From the moment you wake up, to the moment you rest your head at night, everything is up to you; your thoughts, your perceptions, your emotions, your reactions. You alone have the power to determine what something means. You can make changes that will dramatically alter the course of your life, simply by looking at things differently.

I have poured myself into these pages and opened up about my life and experiences in the sincere hope that it will help you experience the same breakthroughs I have and find the same true happiness.

From my heart, thank you. The fact that you are reading this book means so much to me. I have come to believe that we owe it to others to make a difference by sharing what we learn, and that's precisely what I'm doing. If just one reader is able to transform their life by reading these words, then this has all been worthwhile.

To living a full life,

Introduction: Triggering Event

———•———

That was the moment. It had come. I had reached the end of the road. I was done. I had finally broken. I'd wondered when it would happen; how it would feel when it did. I never knew my limits until then.

I collapsed in a heap in the stairwell of my office building.

Feelings unlike anything I'd experienced overwhelmed me. My skin was burning. Down my arms, my hands, and along the length of my fingers. I remember holding my hands up in front of my face to see if they were actually on fire.

I became acutely aware of my heart rate and breathing, both of which increased rapidly to the point that I was light-headed, shaking uncontrollably and entirely out of control. I was experiencing deeply upsetting thoughts – failure, disaster, and helplessness. These thoughts were going round and around in my head. I imagined losing my job and my home. I imagined my long-term girlfriend leaving me. I imagined those closest to me being ashamed and disappointed in me. I even imagined never being able to work again and filing for bankruptcy. The more I focused on these thoughts, the more intense the panic became, and the more severe the physical symptoms.

I now know that was a nervous breakdown, or a severe "panic attack", or whatever you want to call it. No, I'm not talking about the kind of "panic" a little boy experiences when he's away from home for the first time and misses his mom; I'm talking about a full-blown meltdown. An extreme physiological response to prolonged psychological pain.

As the overwhelming feelings peaked, suddenly, there was nothing. Utter nothingness. For a moment, all the symptoms stopped. I had finally let go, physically and emotionally. I don't know if my eyes were open or closed. All I can tell you is that I was wholly disconnected from the real world. Living, for a short time, in my mind alone. No sound. No feeling. Nothing.

Then an image formed in front of me. A beautiful picture of a tropical island. Nothing but palm trees, white sand, clear ocean water, blue skies, and sunshine. Maybe this was my "happy place". Don't ask me why I went there, but I did. I genuinely felt like I was there. I felt the warmth of the sun on my body and the soothing sensation of the sand under my feet. Despite the harrowing experience leading up to this point, this moment was beautiful and calming. Complete surrender. Like I had handed over control entirely. I was at the mercy of whoever, or whatever, was at the helm. And I didn't care.

———•———

The aftermath of the "event" was not fun. Initially, I was like a vegetable. I'm pretty sure all my functions worked fine; I just didn't want to *do* anything. I remember sitting at home, curled up in a ball, for hours on end, just taking in my surroundings. I had little interest in interacting with anyone or anything. I have no idea what I looked like, but I imagine there were moments when I was sat there with my mouth wide open, drooling.

Pretty quickly – within 24-48 hours – I was up and about, talking and interacting with those around me. My speech was slurred and my vocabulary was restricted. You know when you've had too much to drink the night before and the following morning it's like you've lost about 50 I.Q. points? It was just like that, with tiredness from the episode thrown in as well.

I sought medical advice. I was offered medication, which I politely declined. The right answer for me was not drugs. Instead, it was to see a counselor and work through my emotional and psychological difficulties. We analyzed in detail the circumstances that led up to this event. Thinking through how I interpret certain situations, how I react to the behavior of others around me, my insatiable desire to please, and how I was fixated on what others thought of me. Making sense of these issues helped a lot.

I recall a particularly tough conversation I had with my counselor during one of our sessions. She was lovely. Very calm, compassionate and caring. On this particular day, she pushed me pretty hard. I remember saying,

"I just need to recover from this and I'll be fine."

She said,

"Recover? What do you mean, recover? This isn't the kind of thing you just *recover* from. You need to make changes in your life; otherwise, you'll soon have a repeat performance."

That statement hit me like a freight train. I totally understood. The external influences that pushed me to breaking point had subsided (for now). But that didn't mean they wouldn't come around again. There was always going to be another time-pressured project at work. Another relationship challenge to navigate. Another significant life decision to work through.

It became obvious to me that I needed to make changes. Significant changes. Changes to how I see the world and changes to the way I think. Otherwise, there was no doubt I would experience the same thing again. And who knows how much worse it would be the second time around?

All I thought was important at that time was my work. I felt like no one could argue with me being unavailable because of a work call or emergency. Work had become what defined me. I was focused on proving myself, pleasing people and pushing forward aimlessly in my career.

I was validated only by those around me, telling me I was a good person, and doing well. I was fueled solely by praise at work, not a passion for what I was doing. I was focused only on the challenges in front of me and things I didn't have and wanted, not the incredible successes I had already achieved and the fantastic gifts I enjoyed every day.

I was locked up inside, trapped between not wanting to do what I was doing or be who I was being, and thinking there was no other way. I was trapped in a metaphorical prison cell – the walls my mental and emotional blocks – and all I could see in front of me were the bars of the door holding me inside.

It was time to figure out what was actually important to me and move towards it. It was time to find new ways and develop new strategies to change the way I think and feel. It was time to find the tools I needed to break out of my cell and be free. It was time to escape from prison.

PART I:

SIZING YOUR PRISON CELL

———◆———

"Inner peace begins the moment you choose not to allow another person or event to control your emotions."

– Pema Chodron

LOCKED UP

———•———

The constant stress, pressure and expectations at work are brutal. You move from one crisis to the next. You're always rushing around and feeling short on time. It feels like nothing you do is good enough and you live in constant fear of letting someone, everyone, down.

All you see in front of you is the next demand on your time and the work piling up. You are always thinking a short period ahead, trying to anticipate the next problem, and worrying about the next issue before it comes up.

You have that sick feeling in the pit of your stomach most of the day. You're going faster and faster and pushing yourself harder and harder because you think that's how you can escape the feeling.

In the few lucid moments you occasionally have between crises, you question what you're doing and why you're doing it. You zoom out and see the bigger picture, allowing yourself hope that there's something better, and you indulge yourself – just for a moment – by daydreaming and allowing yourself to believe that someday it will all be worth it.

Then you snap back to your current reality of responding to emails, checking spreadsheets, reviewing reports, and updating slide decks. It's incredible that you haven't yet cracked under pressure and that you've kept it up this long!

You're trapped, and you HAVE to go to work every day – there is no alternative. Despite how much you really don't want to. You wake up each day dreading what you have to face. Your days at the office or on a client's site run from crisis to crisis, fire drill to fire drill, and you can't catch a break.

You feel you have to arrive at the office by a particular time otherwise someone, somewhere will notice and make a note of it. You feel like you're burning political capital every time you take a vacation day or leave early for an appointment. You feel like you can't go home until the boss leaves. You are, in many ways, imprisoned. Beholden to others. Not in command of your own time. You must make a change. You simply can't go on like this. It's not sustainable.

If you don't know whether to change positions at work, move to a new company, or quit your job altogether, then this book is for you. Believe it or not, the beauty of your situation is that you don't need to decide right now. What you need to do is put things in perspective and shift your focus.

You see, we are all working so hard to prove ourselves in the eyes of those around us, particularly our employers and those closest to us. All the money and success in the world isn't going to satisfy an insatiable desire to please. What will, is realizing, profoundly *knowing*, that you are already enough.

This so-called freedom that we all seek is available to us all right now. It has nothing to do with the amount of money we earn or the size of our bank balances; it's entirely free of charge. It's only down to *your* perspective on life and how *you* choose to see who you are.

It's your perception of all these seemingly stressful events and circumstances which is fueling a genuine feeling of imprisonment. I believe that how you're feeling has very little to do with the physical reality in which you find yourself. It's how you perceive and react to the things going on around you that is causing your pain.

The solution isn't to change your position at work, move to a new company, or quit your job altogether – although one of those will ultimately be the case for many of you – the solution is to change your mindset and shift your focus to look at your circumstances differently.

You need to fix what's on the inside and lay the foundation for living a full and happy life no matter what goes on around you. Then everything else will fall into place.

When a tree is covered in rotten fruit, you don't look at the fruit and think that's the problem. You know that the tree is diseased and that there's an issue on the inside, at the root of the tree.

Your outer world, and everything you experience day to day, is simply a reflection of your inner world. If your external world is not what you want it to be – and I'm pretty sure that's the case otherwise you wouldn't be reading this – then you need to work on your inner self before making career decisions.

I'm going to show you the tools you need to break out of your glamorous prison and live the life you want. A life filled with positivity, gratitude, abundance, and joy, no matter what is going on around you.

Everything you need to find and enjoy freedom exists within you. Breaking out of prison is an inside job.

Are you ready to escape?

BREAKING FREE

———•———

I used to be miserable. Gut-wrenchingly miserable. I felt empty inside, like I was on a treadmill with no (apparent) way to get off. I had lots and lots of things going for me: meaningful relationships, good health, a high paying job, a beautiful home. Yet, there was a huge void inside me. I had no idea what it was. This must have been incredibly difficult for those closest to me to understand and accept. I had so much going for me and so much to be grateful for – yet I was miserable.

Relationships have always been hugely important to me, and relationships in my life have always been excellent. So, clearly, relationships were not the problem. In fact, my misery had nothing to do with those around me or even the events and circumstances of my life and career. My pain had everything to do with me on the inside.

I didn't want to lose what I had, but I wanted so much more out of life. I wanted to know what I was supposed to be doing. I wanted to know why I was here. I wanted to know how to live a full life. Going to work every day and looking forward to evenings, weekends, and one or two vacations a year just didn't make sense to me anymore. There HAD to be something bigger. A vision for my life. A purpose pulling me forward.

The start of my journey of personal development came when I asked these big questions and actually expected answers for the first time. From feelings of emptiness, I was reaching for something. Anything.

I recall the day things changed for me like it was yesterday. I was at Orlando International Airport (MCO) waiting to board a flight home after a week-long work conference. I was feeling the lowest of lows; horribly down and totally lost.

I knew I wasn't doing what I was supposed to be doing, and I knew I wasn't fulfilling my mission (whatever that was). I knew I needed to make a change and do something completely different. Yet all I could see in front of me was a backlog of work emails and a mounting to-do list of unpleasant tasks.

Sat there, working away on my computer and feeling sorry for myself, I couldn't stop thinking about how much I hated what I was doing. It wasn't fulfilling to me anymore – just a means to an end. Every email frustrated me. Every tap on the keyboard made me uncomfortable. Every click of the computer mouse made me feel emptier inside. I wanted to scream; like a caged animal. At one point, I'm pretty sure I had my head in my hands, shaking my head, fantasizing about all the possible ways I could get away from it all.

It's quite sad when you think about it. Especially when I had so much to be grateful for. Still, my heart was aching and, for the first time, out of desperation, I decided I was going to make some changes. I was unclear about what or how – I just knew this was a turning point.

Sat in the middle of the terminal by the boarding gates, I was surrounded by restaurants, bars and souvenir stores, with lots of people coming and going. Suddenly I got the urge to look up and, in the distance, I saw a woman walking through the terminal towards me. I felt a powerful attraction. No, not like I had the *hots* for her; like I was supposed to see her and I was waiting in anticipation for something to happen. It was weird.

Of all the seats to choose, she decided to come over to the sofa directly opposite me. She asked if anyone was sitting there.

I smiled politely and said that there wasn't.

I noticed she was carrying a lot of bags. As she sat down, she dropped them on the sofa either side of her and made a comment about how heavy they were.

I thought nothing of it and carried on with what I was doing, but I continued to watch her like a kid keeping one eye on the television when he's supposed to be doing his homework.

After a few seconds of silence, lots and lots more complaining in my head about my work, and more feelings of anger and frustration, my new companion said, "Do you like reading?"

I looked up, a little surprised by the question, especially from a complete stranger, and said, "Sure, I like reading."

She said, "I have a book for you" and reached into one of her bags.

She pulled out a book and handed it to me.

I quickly read the back and saw that it was a personal development book written by a well-known author who is well respected in that field. The book was explicitly about reinventing your career and life.

Interesting.

I'm in the middle of an airport terminal, thinking about how I need to make significant changes in my life, then some random stranger walks in and hands me a book about reinventing yourself. Needless to say, she had my attention at this point!

We got to talking and I opened up a little about feeling lost in life and what I thought I wanted. She explained about the personal development journey she was on and the transformational seminar she'd just attended that weekend.

I was a little weirded out by the "coincidence" of all this, though quite hopeful that this might, in some way, be the first step towards creating a life of fulfillment.

I must have looked a little shocked, and I know I made a comment or two about how I was surprised that this had happened. Especially given I was sat there thinking about this very topic and looking for answers when the lady showed up.

I'll never forget what she said next. She leaned forward, looked me straight in the eyes, and said,

"You know we met for a reason, right?"

That comment sent (nice) chills down my back. I've never been religious, and I certainly didn't have the spiritual beliefs then that I have now, but it was abundantly clear to me that this was a sign of some sort. It could not have been more obvious. It was like a metaphorical slap in the face; a real wake-up call!

This encounter started me on a journey of discovery. I decided then and there I was going to make a change. No more blindly following the rules. No more doing everything I thought others wanted me to. No more following the herd because that's what everyone else does. I promised myself: it's my life and I'm going to make something of it. I'm going to find my passion and deliver it to the world.

I began feverishly reading personal development books, studying meditation and other spiritual endeavors, focusing on health and wellness with dedication, attending mastermind groups and weekend seminars, and visualizing what I wanted for my life like never before.

Every step of the way I learned something new and I took giant leaps forward in how I was feeling. I turned the knowledge I accumulated along the way and the life-changing lessons I experienced into "tools" that enabled me to break out of my emotional prison and claim true freedom.

These are the tools I'm going to share with you so that you can do the same.

LIFE ON THE OUTSIDE

———•———

Today, I am truly happy. I am married to the same amazing woman. I have the same wonderful "fur baby". I live in the same beautiful home. I am surrounded by the same loving family and friends. I work every day with many of the same bright, intellectual people. I enjoy the same food and drink. Nothing (on the outside) has changed. Yet, my life is entirely different.

I learned that life is right now, it's not later. Life is not when you get a pay rise, or when you get recognized at work, or when you make partner in your firm. It's not when you go on vacation somewhere luxurious and exclusive. It's not when you move into a bigger house. It's not when you have more money in your bank account. Life is right now!

What if I told you that life isn't *happening* to you, it's *responding* to you? What if I told you that every aspect of your life is down to you? That you make the call on how your life unfolds based on what you give out?

Let that sink in for a moment.

It means that how you think and feel at any moment is more important than anything else – because how you think and feel is actually creating what you experience in life.

If you knew this to be true, wouldn't you immediately change the way you think, speak and act? Would you be more grateful for everything in your life? Would you be more amazed every day by all the incredible things happening around you?

Life is not about what happens to you, it's about how you choose to respond. It's not what goes on around you, but how you react that matters. If you change your focus, everything else will change. Things will begin to work out for you.

This is the astonishing reality of how life really works. Once, I didn't understand this. I had no idea. I didn't always know how the world worked. I used to allow events and circumstances determine how I felt. Now I know that *how I feel* is what determines the events and circumstances around me.

It wasn't long ago that I woke up and, for the first time, saw the world for what it was: a giant playground. We really do have the power to determine our experiences from moment to moment.

We shape our reality with our thoughts and our beliefs. If we start to pay attention to how we feel, and we direct our thoughts, happiness can be ours immediately.

Realize that nothing is more important than how you feel right now, and you will be amazed by the shift in your life.

Most of us haven't even scratched the surface of what life has to offer. Life has the potential to be whatever you want it to be. Literally anything. You just need to have the courage to dream and the audacity to believe. Once you truly know what you want, the means with which to obtain it will follow. If only we would spend more time thinking about what we want and having faith that everything is playing out just the way it's supposed to.

You are meant to have an amazing life. You are meant to have everything you love and desire. Your work is intended to be exciting, and you are meant to accomplish all the things you want to achieve. Your relationships with your family and friends are meant to wonderful. You're meant to have all the money you need to live a full life. You're meant to laugh and feel joy all the time. You're meant to feel secure and confident in the face of adversity. You're meant to feel good and love yourself. You're meant to experience challenges that make you grow, and you're meant to know how to overcome these challenges when you're faced with them.

I don't think we were born to be in emotional pain all the time. We weren't born to live a life where moments of joy are infrequent. We weren't born to drag ourselves to work five or more days a week, with brief moments of happiness in-between. We weren't born to live with limited energy, feeling exhausted at the end of each workday. We weren't born to worry or be afraid of what others think of us. We weren't born to be miserable. What would be the point?

The heart was made to swell and jump and stir; that's a fact. I think we are all meant to experience life to its fullest and have the opportunity to enjoy everything that we want.

I love the idea that the life of your dreams, with everything you want to be, have, or do, is just around the corner. All you have to do is make a commitment to live the life you want to live and to making your dreams reality. This doesn't mean changing who you are overnight, it means focusing on what you want in all areas of your life and making it happen, one dream at a time.

Life is not about the destination, it's about the journey. When we get something we've been striving for, we rarely remain satisfied. The purpose has never been receiving everything you want; the aim has always been the way you feel moment by moment, because that's what life is. The things are just the bait. Chasing after things forces us to grow. That's what fulfills us: *growth*. It's the journey not the rewards that matter to us, and the bumps along the road are not pushing us off course – they're not wrong – they're part of the course.

Join me to learn the tools you need to break free and start living a full life. They changed my life. I genuinely believe they will change *yours* and enable you to escape from the prison of your mind.

PART II:

THE TOOLS NEEDED TO BREAK FREE

———•———

"Liberate yourself from negative emotions and transform your life."

– Judith Orloff

INSTRUCTIONS

Part II – The Tools Needed To Break Free, is structured to include a stand-alone chapter for each of the ten tools.

We will go through each tool in turn, introducing it with stories and metaphors. Then I will guide you through the material with easy-to-understand concepts, personal stories and empowering examples.

Each tool chapter includes a summary of the fundamentals covered in that chapter, which will serve as a valuable reference for you, and contains one or more exercises to help you put the tool into practice.

The exercises are designed to help you progress. I ask that you be careful about using the three most dangerous words anyone can say when it comes to personal development: *I know that.*

Those words are not your friend.

They come from a place of false confidence. In other words, from a place of fear. As soon as you say, *I know that*, you shut off your ability to learn and grow. *I know that* is what makes you skip exercises, only do part of an exercise, or perhaps not write something down when the exercise calls for writing. My heartfelt suggestion is that you remain open-minded and follow the exercises in this book.

I can't wait for you to experience amazing changes in your life!

BOOK BONUSES

To best support you going forward, as you put these tools into practice, I have created some bonus online content for you.

Visit **www.shapingreality.com/book-bonuses** and download the book bonuses for free.

TOOL #1: GRATITUDE

———•———

"No duty is more urgent than that of returning thanks."

– Saint Ambrose

TOOL #1: GRATITUDE

———•———

> grat · i · tude
>
> *noun*
>
> the quality of being thankful; readiness to show appreciation for and to return kindness.

Do you have any idea of the power of gratitude? Gratitude is like the sledgehammer of tools. If you use this right and make it part of who you are, you will absolutely crush it in life.

By gratitude, I don't just mean saying "thanks" when someone holds the door for you. I mean the deep, moving, emotional glow you feel in your heart when you are truly grateful for something or someone.

A sincere "thank you" instead of an automatic, "Oh, thanks," makes you feel pretty good, right?

I'm sure there have been moments in your life that you can reflect on, that involved strong feelings of gratitude.

Maybe after a beautiful time spent with friends, you're feeling really good and reflecting on just how lovely your friends are. How they make you smile when you think of them. Or sometimes when you're together how you laugh so hard that you can't breathe. Thinking of them brings back the history from years of friendship and a lifetime of memories together. You're filled with pride and appreciation to have such extraordinary and meaningful people in your life. It's almost overwhelming; it's moving. Maybe you even choke up a little, or you get goosebumps. That is gratitude; it's intense and it comes from the heart.

Imagine you could induce that feeling about anything and everything in your life. Well, you can. You just need to shift your perspective onto the seemingly little things in your life. Because, when you look around, this life is amazing. Your experiences in life are gifts. Waking up in the morning with the whole day ahead of you is remarkable when you think about it.

Why am I telling you this? Because when I started to be grateful – and I mean really thankful for everything – my life became amazing. Exciting new opportunities presented themselves. The very best of the people around me showed up. I felt healthy, physically and emotionally. I felt happy for the first time. And, I'm sure this will excite you, money started flowing into my life like never before.

Let's explore the attitude of gratitude.

THE ATTITUDE OF GRATITUDE

Dating back thousands of years to the earliest recordings of mankind, the power of gratitude was preached and practiced. History is laden with famous figures who practiced gratitude, and whose achievements put them amongst the most exceptional human beings who have ever lived. The scientists, philosophers, inventors, discoverers and prophets who practiced gratitude reaped its rewards. Yet the power of appreciation is unrecognized by most people today.

The attitude of gratitude is far more than lukewarm advice. Stacks of recent books and articles tell us that people who are grateful in their daily lives are more likely to get along with others, sleep better, be less depressed, and have better overall physical health. They also achieve more, have more friends, and avoid burnout. Gratitude might just be the healthiest emotion of all.

We can actually study the brain and see that when people are grateful for something, specific parts of the brain that represent memory light up. The myelin sheaths of the neurosynaptic connections around the memory of the thing we're grateful for, become thicker. The electrical impulse between those connections in your brain actually becomes stronger. The result is engaging the brain to find more of that which you are grateful for.

In other words, gratitude is a way to signal your brain that you want more of what you experienced. Therefore, you have more ideas in alignment with the experiences you're grateful for. You begin to see things in your life similar to that which you are thankful for – things that were always there – and you begin to attract even more experiences, people, and resources to be grateful for.

Doesn't that sound like a pretty good strategy?

IT'S ALL ABOUT FOCUS

It's easy to focus on what's wrong with your life. Given how busy and complicated our lives can be, we can say with almost complete certainty that there is at least one thing going "wrong" at any point in time. But what's right in your life is also available to focus on at all times. Which one makes more sense to focus on?

Think of this question like yard work. No matter how much time you spend pulling out the weeds, they always come back, right? Then stop focusing on the weeds and instead focus on the flowers. I hear you: the weeds are still there so you must continue to pull them out, right? No, doesn't it make more sense to tend the flowers than pay attention to the weeds? If you dedicate your time and energy to watering the flowers, soon they will grow big enough to block the weeds from the sun. It's merely a matter of shifting your focus.

Engaging the power of gratitude is as simple as shifting your focus to an appreciation for what you *do have,* rather than complaining about what you *don't have.* You can take all your negative thoughts and emotions about one thing and swap them for an appreciation of something else. You will feel better immediately.

THE POWER OF GRATITUDE

The best way out of any unwanted situation is gratitude. No matter who you are, where you are, or your current circumstances, gratitude has the potential to change your life in an instant. Because it has the power to change your feelings and, therefore, what you experience in any given moment.

You can't feel bad about something and be grateful at the same time. You can't experience negative emotions towards anything and be grateful at the same time.

If you're thinking, "I don't have enough money," "I can't do that," "I don't want to be sick" or "I don't have enough time," then you will only experience those feelings and acknowledge those events in your life.

If you're grateful… "I love my home", "I'm so grateful for the people I work with", "I got a big tax refund this year" or "I had the best dinner with my friends this weekend" …then you are focused on and will continue to enjoy those things in your life.

We've all heard the sayings, "What goes around comes around", "You reap what you sow" and "You get what you give" All of those are describing the same thing: your experiences are determined by what you give out.

If you know this to be true, why would you be anything but grateful?

HOW GRATEFUL ARE YOU?

I'm going to tell you a secret: you won't get more of anything until you're grateful for what you have. If you want more money, be grateful for the money you have. If you want better relationships, be grateful for the relationships you have. If you want a better job, be grateful for the job you have. If you want to feel better physically, be grateful for the health you already enjoy.

You can tell right now how grateful you are by looking at the major areas of your life: money and finances, career or business, relationships, health and wellness, recreation, etc.

In the areas of your life that are going particularly well, I guarantee you'll find a correlation between how grateful you are and your current results.

To me, it's simple: if you're not grateful for what you have, then you cannot receive more of anything in return.

When you're not grateful for your health, your relationships, your joy, and your financial situation, then you are responsible for why things are not getting better.

Relationships have always been significant to me. I'm glad to say that they have always been outstanding. Even before I understood the importance and power of gratitude, I would often reflect on the loved ones in my life and feel deeply grateful. I can recount numerous times when I have been moved almost to tears just thinking about the supportive and loving people around me. No wonder relationships have always been and continue to be sincere and meaningful in my life!

Conversely, I have always wanted more money. Despite being what most would consider financially stable, I often felt worried, disappointed, or jealous of others about money. Those feelings came from my lack of gratitude for the money I had. Now I am incredibly grateful for the money in my life. I don't worry about spending, and I give huge thanks every time I swipe my credit card, acknowledging how incredible it is that I don't have to worry about that action.

Guess what? I now have more money in my life than ever before. Money comes to me from unexpected sources, and moneymaking opportunities present themselves every day. Coincidence? I think not.

THE MAGIC WORDS

To experience the enormous impact of gratitude, you must practice it every day and make it a way of life for you.

As you focus on being grateful for everything in your life, you may well start to notice why certain things have gone wrong in your life so far. I certainly did.

The words *thank you* are so, so important. To live in gratitude, *thank you* must become the two words you deliberately say and feel more than any other words. They need to become part of who you are. They are the link between where you are today and where you want to be in any area of your life. They are the magic words.

When you make appreciation core to your life, you will find yourself feeling more and more in love with everyone and everything around you. Taking action will require less effort and overcoming challenges will be more comfortable.

Maybe you are someone who already notices what you have. But do you take the time to *feel* deeply grateful for what you have? If not, then I urge you to be thankful for what you have already. Focus on being thankful for everything in your life. Appreciation for what you have will make way for new levels of emotional well-being and wealth in your life.

The objective of practicing gratitude is to intentionally feel it as much as you can. Think and say the words, *thank you*. The more intentionally you think and say *thank you*, the more grateful you will feel. The more you think and feel gratitude, the more you will get back.

When you see how little practice it takes, how easy it is to make it part of your day, and when you start to see results in how much better you feel, you will never turn back. A deep feeling of gratitude is where joy can be found.

Gratitude will make way for so much more to come into your life. Try it and see what happens. You will be amazed.

FUNDAMENTALS

- Gratitude is an intense feeling; it comes from your heart.

- What's wrong in your life is always available to you and so is what's right. Which one makes more sense to focus on?

- The best way out of any unwanted situation is gratitude. It has the power to change your feelings and, therefore, what you experience in any given moment.

- You can tell now how grateful you are by looking at the major areas of your life. In the areas that are going particularly well, you will find a correlation between how grateful you are and your current results.

- To experience the enormous impact of gratitude, you must practice it every day and make it a way of life for you.

- The words *thank you* are so, so important. They must become the two words you deliberately say and feel more than any other words.

- The objective of practicing gratitude is to intentionally feel it as much as you can. The more intentionally you think and say thank you, the more grateful you will feel and the more you will get back.

EXERCISES

1. Counting your blessings

Growing up, I often heard people say, "Count your blessings." I thought it sounded like a beautiful thing to do; to reflect on the things in your life that you're grateful for. I had no idea that counting your blessings is actually one of the most powerful practices you can master.

When you're grateful for what you have, no matter how big or small, you will feel much more happiness and joy in your life, and you will see those things increase.

Count your blessings as early as you can in your day – preferably, first thing in the morning. Do this by making a simple list of ten things in your life for which you are grateful. These can be any ten things you want: a person, an object, a situation, or an event. Write your list by hand, perhaps in a special journal or notebook, or type it on a computer or smartphone.

It's crucial to think about *why* you are grateful for each of the ten things. When you contemplate the reason *why* you're thankful, you feel gratitude more deeply. So, for each item on your list, write the reason you're grateful for it.

This is the structure I follow when I write my list:

- I am so happy and grateful for _____, because_____.

- I am deeply grateful for _____, because _____.

- I feel so blessed to have _____, because _____.

- Thank you so much for _____, because _____.

Here are a few examples from one of my daily lists:

- I am so happy and grateful for the precious relationships in my life because I am surrounded by love and warmth.

- I am blessed to have a healthy body because I am resilient and heal quickly.

- Thank you for all the money in my life because I can enjoy so many luxuries and share them with others.

- With all my heart, thank you for my beautiful puppy because he is pure joy!

If you direct your gratitude toward someone or something, it may help you to feel gratitude even more deeply. I'm not pushing any religious or spiritual beliefs here. It could be God, the Universe, life, infinite intelligence, whatever or whomever you believe in.

Look closely at your life, all you have received, all that you have to look forward to, and all that you experience every day. I'm confident you will see that there is a lot for which you can be grateful.

Here's the list of areas of life that I use, to serve as guidance for you on where to look for blessings:

- Money and personal finances
- Career or business
- Relationships
- Health and wellness
- Personal and spiritual development
- Recreation and play
- Personal environment
- Service and contribution

I expect you to feel better and happier each time you complete this practice. How good you feel after the exercise is a reasonable measure of how much gratitude you felt during it. Some days you will feel good quickly and easily, and other days it will take a little more effort. Please stick with it.

By counting your blessings every day, you will notice more and more of a difference. Do this for at least ten days and see how you feel.

There's one more thing I like to do in this area. It came to me when I started to notice things changing. I highly recommend you keep a list of all the good things that happen. Like pleasant surprises, coincidences, and unexpected gifts or good news.

Not only is it beautiful to be aware and take notice of what starts to happen as a result of your gratitude, but writing a list is a form of gratitude itself. This adds to your practice because you're acknowledging what's happening and appreciating it.

Here are a few examples of lovely things that have happened in my life:

- Driving home from work, I made a split-second decision to turn off the highway early, which avoided an unexpected traffic jam.

- I enjoyed an unexpected free drink in my favorite coffee shop for no reason at all.

- I pulled into the only available parking space right outside the store I was visiting, at the precise moment I needed it.

- An unexpected upgrade to business class on an international flight.

- A friend showed up with a can of rare craft beer that I had wanted to try for years, without me ever telling him I wanted it.

I am deliberately listing things you may think are "small." There have been a considerable number of "big" things that have happened for which I am eternally grateful. The point is that I want you to see how beautiful and joyous the seemingly little things are. It makes you feel good to acknowledge them and appreciate them. It makes life fun and exciting. You never know what gifts are coming your way next. That, to me, is a beautiful state of mind.

Summary instructions

1. Make a list of **ten** things in your life for which you are grateful.

2. Write *why* you are thankful for each item.

3. Go back over your list and read it aloud. At the end of each item, say the words, *thank you*, and feel gratitude as much as you can.

4. Repeat the first three steps every morning for at least **ten** days.

5. Keep a list of all the good things that happen, like surprising coincidences and unexpected gifts or good news.

Book bonuses

To help make this process easier and more impactful, I have created a template Gratitude Journal for you which is available for download.

Visit **www.shapingreality.com/book-bonuses** and download it for free.

2. Shine your love light

Some people find the concept of gratitude challenging to employ. Especially when they are staring down the proverbial barrel of something they do not want.

There's another way to look at this and to help "activate" the wonderful feeling of gratitude: Love.

If you can't conjure up the feeling of gratitude, simply focus instead on making sure you are always giving love. I know it sounds weird but hear me out.

Love has been talked about and written about since the beginning of time by great thinkers, philosophers, prophets, and leaders.

I'm talking about much more than loving your family, friends, and favorite possessions. I'm certainly talking about more than the "in-love" experience you have at the start of an intimate relationship. I'm talking about love as more than just a feeling. I'm talking about love as a force that moves you.

When you stop to help someone carry their suitcase up the subway stairs. Or you stop to give someone helpful directions. Or maybe you hand someone your parking stub with thirty minutes left on it. Even when you take a few moments in your day to compliment someone on how they are dressed... you feel good, right?

You are doing that out of love. Not love like you want to jump into bed with the person. Not love like you have a long-standing relationship with them. I mean love like the inherent, natural desire to do something for others and to be of service. The feeling is very similar to that of the warm glow of gratitude we feel in our hearts.

Love draws people to one another, it pulls one person into the field of science and another into sports, and it drives people toward different music, cuisines, or hobbies. Love attracts you to your favorite things and places, and it draws you to your friends and the people you care about most.

Without love, you wouldn't feel anything. You wouldn't be attracted to another person, a particular home, a car, a job, a song, a style of clothing, or anything, because it's through attraction that you feel love.

In the state of love, you project positive energy. Love is one of the highest emotional states you can experience.

Love is powerful and it flows wherever you focus your attention. I think of it as a warm glow beaming out of me towards someone, or something, when I choose to shine my love light.

We make contact with so many people in our everyday lives. Think of the different people you interact with each day and how many of them help you, do something for you, or provide you with some kind of service.

- The people working in stores, malls and restaurants are all making your shopping and dining experiences enjoyable.

- The people working in the transport system on trains, planes and buses are making sure you reach your destination safely and on time.

- The people working for utility companies are making sure that gas, electricity and water are flowing to your home.

- The people working in your local town are fixing potholes in the road or cleaning the streets of leaves and debris.

- The people working in your offices from administrative staff to cleaners are helping you do your job.

There are a staggering number of people whose efforts benefit you each day. This exercise is about you shining your love light on those people.

Sit down with a particular journal or notebook, or type on a computer or smartphone, and recall when someone in the service industry went out of their way for you. Make a list of at least ten instances where someone has performed an act of service for you and send them that warm glow of gratitude and love. Picture each moment in your mind. Relive the experience and send that person love and appreciation.

Now look for every opportunity you can shine your love light from today onwards. Thank at least ten people who perform different services you benefit from today. This could be by thanking them directly or by mentally and emotionally recognizing them. Feel thankful for the service they have provided, no matter how big or small.

When you interact with someone mean or unpleasant in any way, it becomes more challenging to shine your love light on them. Be thankful for them and give them love *anyway* – you have no idea what they are going through. I am sure they didn't wake up with the sole intention of seeking you out and being mean to you. Go easy on them; we have all been there. Your gratitude and love should not be dependent on someone else's behavior and, you never know, your kindness might just turn things around for them.

Summary instructions

1. Make a list of at least **ten** instances where someone has performed an act of service for you. Relive the moment and send them that warm glow of gratitude and love.

2. Thank at least **ten** people who perform different services you benefit from today. This could be by thanking them directly or by recognizing them in your mind.

TOOL #2: BELIEF

———•———

*"The best time to plant a tree was 20 years ago.
The second best time is now."*

– Chinese Proverb

TOOL #2: BELIEF

---·---

> be · lief
>
> *noun*
>
> 1. an acceptance that a statement is true or that something exists.
>
> 2. trust, faith, or confidence in someone or something.

When I lived in Manhattan, New York, I was often staggered by the amount of construction going on all over the city. I'd often look at the buildings along my most regular routes – on my way to work, to a coffee shop, to one of my favorite restaurants. Everything would be familiar until one day a building was gone. Just disappeared! Demolished in no time at all. Ready to make way for new construction.

After the initial demolition, it seemed to take forever for anything to happen. You'd see a flurry of activity every day on the site where the building once stood. Delivery vehicles were coming and going, cranes moving materials around, and construction workers crawling all over like ants. Yet apparently not much was happening. You'd hear the jackhammers and power saws late into the night and in the early hours of the morning. It seemed like the site was sinking into the ground rather than growing.

Months and months would go by, and there was nothing to show for it. I would think, "I thought they were building a new sixty-story apartment building, where is it?"

Then, one day, boom! Two stories built, then five, then ten, then twenty. Before you knew it, the entire building was framed and standing tall in the New York City skyline. What happened? Well, the vast majority of the time was spent on the foundations. The base of the building was strong and deep. It had to be, to support such a magnificent structure.

Why am I using this analogy? Because you are setting the foundations for building whatever it is you want in your life when you install empowering beliefs. The right beliefs are critical to achieving your dreams.

These beliefs will drive you in the right direction, find evidence to support your goals and ambitions, and govern your behavior and actions to create what you want.

Let's talk about a hypothetical college graduate in a large professional services firm. Imagine an overly keen, entry-level associate in your company promoted into the partnership, or appointed to the board, within two years of joining the organization. Given signing rights and executive decision-making authority.

How well do you think that would play out? How long before a disaster would strike?

Experience is the foundation here. Being calm and measured under pressure. Having the knowledge to deal with almost any situation and, perhaps more importantly, having the courage to walk the halls and ask for help when you don't know the answer. Unafraid to hit pause and take the time you need to think through an issue and make the right call. Comfortable to stand up to the crowd and do the right thing, even when it's unpopular. That is the foundation for a successful executive, not just raw ambition and willingness to work long hours.

Do you see my point? Whatever it is you are trying to build it must have a firm footing. Work on the foundation first – your beliefs.

YOUR SUBCONSCIOUS MIND

Your subconscious mind determines the level of success in all areas of your life. It's that simple.

Even if you say that you want to achieve something, if your subconscious mind is not in alignment, then you won't get there. Your subconscious mind will always win.

You may think and say, "I really want to be a senior manager. I am ready to get promoted." But, if in your subconscious mind you really believe, "I definitely want to be promoted to senior manager, but I'm not sure they think I'm experienced enough yet" then this dream will not become a reality for you.

The key to understanding this fact is the following: we do not create what we want, we create what we believe. It is all about *belief*. What you believe manifests in your life. There's a direct correlation between positive thinking and positive outcomes. A negative mindset will always give you a negative life. A positive mindset will always give you a positive life.

For example, if you are experiencing financial difficulty or having trouble achieving the level of wealth that you want to, I am willing to bet that it's because you have limiting beliefs about money.

If you say you want one thing, but you believe something else, you are blocking yourself from achieving success in that area. This is true about any area of your life.

Underlying (subconscious) uncertainty and doubt as a result of disempowering beliefs will drive your thinking and actions accordingly.

Some call this a belief system. Some call this programming. Some call this your mental blueprint. The concept is the same: your outer world is simply a "printout" of your inner world. In other words, your subconscious beliefs and habits create your reality.

RETICULAR ACTIVATING SYSTEM

There is something in the brain called the Reticular Activating System. It's a filter in your brain that is applied to the staggering amount of information gathered every moment by your five senses. This filter works constantly, and it's the only thing keeping you from being overwhelmed and overloaded by the unimaginable level of stimuli passing through your senses.

Your brain sees even when you don't. The unconscious processing abilities of the human brain are estimated at 11 million pieces of information per second. Compare that to the estimate for conscious processing: 40 bits of data per second.

Our brain filters all this information down to the narrow band of what we consciously experience. That narrow band is based on what we think is important and relevant. In other words, what we believe. The remaining data gets filtered out and transferred directly to the unconscious parts of the brain.

Have you ever noticed when you're shopping for something, how you see examples of it everywhere? For example, you're considering buying a particular car, then you see so many driving around and parked on the street. Even the specific color you are considering. It's almost like there are more of them than ever before and you see them everywhere, right?

Well, when we set a goal or an intention, we indicate to the Reticular Activating System that anything associated with that is important to us. As a result, the Reticular Activating System goes to work to bring to our attention information and opportunities to help us get there.

Your brain is an electrical device. It outputs energy in the form of waves. These waves interact with vibrations everywhere to manufacture events and circumstances in your life. We've all thought about someone and then they've called us, or we've been reminiscing about someone and they've shown up unexpectedly in the grocery store. It's not luck. There is a connection between our localized intelligence and a source of infinite intelligence, and the connection is what we think.

So, it's no wonder we see and experience more of what we think about.

TECHNOLOGY OF THE BRAIN

Let's think about the technology of the brain and tie it into how beliefs work.

You are born with around 100 billion neurons in your brain. These are electrically excitable cells. You are also born with 25 billion synaptic connections. These are the connections between the neurons in the brain.

By the time you are six to seven years old, you still have 100 billion neurons and you go from having 25 billion synaptic connections to over 1 quadrillion. That's 1,000 trillion! That's a lot, right? So, the question is, *what happened?* Basically, you built a massive neural network in your brain.

We have the most incredible data collectors – our five senses. They collect information continuously and send it to our brain through our nervous system. This enables us to perceive what's going on around us. Your brain, like a hard drive, has recorded, moment by moment, every experience you've had.

Let's pretend you are four or five years old and you have experienced your parents arguing about something. You heard them through a closed door. You've recorded all this information and you've recorded the meaning that *you* give to the experience. Maybe you heard them arguing about money, so you decided that money is hard to earn. It's not necessarily true, it's just the meaning you gave to an experience you had when you were four or five years old.

This has been stored in your brain, and it has become part of who you are; part of your belief system. So, in any subsequent moment when you experience something to do with money, your brain says, "What do we know about this thing?" The response that immediately comes back is, "Money is hard to earn." Or, "You can make money, but it doesn't stay around for long." Maybe even, "Money causes arguments" or "Money troubles lead to relationships ending."

We end up living this experience over and over again because of the meaning we attached to it. These limiting beliefs are meanings we associate with experiences we don't even remember anymore. These perpetuate themselves into our present-day reality.

Anywhere you feel stuck, or are experiencing lack in your life, what's likely happened is that you are continuing to live based on a limiting belief.

Limiting beliefs are simply a series of neuro-synaptic connections in your brain that represent your memory of something and the meaning you gave to that experience.

The problem with limiting beliefs is that your brain is a goal-achieving device. It's always trying to bring into reality and prove what you believe. Let's say, for example, you experience something in your life that made you think you were a poor communicator. You will actually *become* a poor communicator as a result.

Moment to moment your brain will be trying to achieve this goal/belief that you are a poor communicator. Perhaps you become confused or misinterpret something, or the words you are trying to say don't come out of your mouth the way you want them to. That's how powerful the brain is – it can actually make you a poor communicator just because it's trying to establish and prove your belief.

HOW BELIEFS AFFECT YOUR LIFE

To appreciate how much your beliefs affect your life, think about the phenomenon that most of us have heard of: the placebo effect.

The placebo effect is a beneficial effect that is produced by a placebo drug or treatment that cannot be attributed to the properties of the placebo itself. It must, therefore, be due to the patient's *belief* that drug or treatment is effective.

For example, giving a sugar pill to someone for a headache when they believe it's aspirin, will often provide relief from the pain even though the sugar pill has no ingredients to reduce pain.

Recent research shows, impressively, that we can get the benefits even when we *know* something is a placebo. Think about that: I can give you a sugar pill for your headache, tell you it's just a sugar pill and, as long as you believe it will work, there's a good chance it will!

After years and years of research we do not fully understand the placebo effect, but it is real, and there is scientific evidence to support the view that *what you believe can change your reality.* Amazing. Just amazing.

COMPLAINING DOESN'T HELP

One of the biggest mistakes I continuously made during my period of misery was focusing on what I did not want.

I would think, "I don't want to be unhappy," "I don't want to feel inadequate like this" or "I don't want to be working all the time."

Clearly, these are negative statements about what I didn't want in my life. I was complaining and the more I complained the worse I felt.

I thought, like most people, that I had a right to complain about the things I didn't like or that weren't going right. Now I know that the things in my life that I didn't like or that weren't going right were due to my complaining!

The problem wasn't that I had a lot to complain about, it was that I didn't understand what I was setting in motion when I complained. The more I complained about what I didn't want, the more I experienced that which

I did not wish. Focusing all the time on how your life sucks means that your mind will work to bring you evidence to prove that your life sucks. Then you'll say "My life sucks" again. And, guess what? Your life will suck!

Ever heard the saying, "perception is reality?" If you think that carries any weight, then hopefully you can see that you can change your reality by changing your perception. Your perception is nothing more than your interpretation and projection based on your beliefs.

You don't necessarily need to understand what's going on in terms of governing your life experience, you just have to know how to work things to your advantage. Look at it this way: do you really understand how electricity works? No, probably not. Does that stop you from switching on a light? No, definitely not.

EVER-IMPROVING STORY

Knowing that your beliefs create your reality gives you the ideal starting point for beginning to enact change, knowing that change will come from uninstalling the limiting beliefs that are keeping you where you are.

You can change your limiting beliefs at the subconscious level, and what you want will then start appearing in your life.

Identify your limiting beliefs and replace them with new, empowering beliefs by dragging them out into the open and realizing what they really are: pain-inducing, life-limiting myths that do not serve you.

Think of your collective beliefs as a story. If you improve the content of the story you tell about you and your life, then you will start to believe, and your life will become an ever-improving story. You can position anything positively and achieve the desired outcome.

For example, you are almost certainly conscious of the additional demands and pressure on you during a busy time at work; perhaps tax season, a financial year-end, or the final stages of a large project. As a result, you will be focused on why you're stressed and the fact that you are feeling immense pressure, a lack of time, and how you would like to get away or get out. That's not going to make you feel any better about the situation. Instead, focus on how you'd like to reach the end of the project and how accomplished you will feel when you do. Think about how great it would feel to have a super-productive day and be surprised at how quickly and easily you complete one of the big scary tasks on your to-do list. Do you see how that gets to the same point, yet it's a different feeling? You are no longer focused on the negative; it's much more positive and empowering.

IDENTIFYING LIMITING BELIEFS

The challenge when it comes to beliefs is that it's difficult sometimes to realize we have them. We have been conditioned over time to accept things without consciously deciding whether they are what we believe to be accurate, right, or sound.

Let me put it this way: we don't make a conscious decision about what we believe. Our beliefs are based on generalizations we make about our past. Given that many of us tend to focus more on painful experiences, more often than not, we form pessimistic beliefs.

Limiting beliefs influence our behavior and affect the action we take. This affects the results we get, which, in turn, reinforce our limiting beliefs. If you continue to tell yourself a story, it will continue to be true. When you change your story, you change your life.

To find that empowering story, we have to deal with our limiting beliefs. It all comes down to a conscious decision to recondition your mind with empowering beliefs.

For example, right now, you may think one of the following:

> *You must have a degree to get a high-paying job.*
> *You must have good genetics to be fit and healthy.*
> *Having a job provides security; working for yourself is risky.*

These are not necessarily facts. Countless, highly successful, highly paid individuals don't have a formal education. There is evidence out there that your genes do not entirely determine your destiny. Ask any successful, self-employed person, and they would say that relying on an employer to pay your salary is the scariest thing there is.

I'm not saying whether any of those are true, right, or good. I'm saying that they are all beliefs. True or not, beliefs are self-fulfilling prophecies. This means that everything in your life is there because your beliefs have, at some point or another, supported its existence.

Our limiting beliefs are keeping us from having what we want in our lives. If you're going to create change in your mindset and outlook, you need to knock the legs out from under these disempowering beliefs.

When you think you're not good enough, you experience a life of feeling inadequate. When you think there's never enough time to get everything done, you will always feel rushed. When you think you're a poor communicator, you'll encounter people not understanding what you're trying to say. None of these experiences are because you're not good enough, or there isn't enough time, or you're a poor communicator. It's because you believe these things to be true. Therefore, you interpret reality in this way to the point where it starts to become your life.

Beliefs aren't facts. They're choices you've made over and over again about something. You get to choose the ones you want to believe, and I highly recommend you choose the ones that serve you!

CHANGING YOUR BELIEFS

So, how do we change limiting beliefs?

Beliefs are *choices*. Think again about my earlier example. You were around five years old and you overheard Mom and Dad arguing about money. It led to you unconsciously concluding that money is hard to make, or leads to problems, or causes arguments.

You made a *choice* that this was the case when you gave it meaning. Over time, at an unconscious level, you have continued to choose to believe this to be true every time you've been faced with the topic of money.

We may not know how to instantaneously believe something new, but we certainly know how to make a choice, right?

I can't tell you how many times in the past I've agonized and stressed myself out leading up to an important presentation or meeting at work.

All these terrible, disempowering thoughts rushed through my mind:

- "I haven't prepared enough for this, and they are going to be able to tell straight away."

- "I'm going to get a question that I can't answer and feel like an idiot."

- "I hate it when the boss looks at me with me disappointment, it makes me feel so inadequate."

Can you relate to thoughts like this?

How about you choose these instead:

- "I am the best person to deliver this presentation, that's why they asked me to."

- "I know more than enough to field any questions that come my way."

- "I can't wait to impress them in there and walk out of the room with my head held high."

Why not? The second list is no more true or false than the first!

Unfortunately, out of habit I think most people choose the lack perspective when it comes to any problematic situation. Instead of looking for evidence of success, happiness and thriving, people see restriction, limitation, and failure. That makes us feel stressed out and under enormous pressure. Tune yourself to see all the choices available to you, and good-feeling experiences will soon dominate your life.

Although it costs nothing to make this mindset shift, the challenge people face is down to their fundamental attitude and outlook. Given that attitude or perspective is governed by beliefs, most people can't even take the smallest steps toward shifting their viewpoint and making changes in their lives because they have limiting beliefs, so they think they can't.

A large part of this depends on educating *you,* so that you give yourself permission to make a different choice whenever you want. Most of us don't think we can because we have so much evidence to support our old beliefs. Your brain has been calibrated to find evidence to support the conclusion you came to over and over again, and to ignore everything else. You must realize this. It's not necessarily true; you merely enrolled your brain to pay attention to it. That's why you have so much evidence to support your current beliefs!

You can choose to believe something else at any time you want. You *can* decide you are good enough, or that you have plenty of time to achieve the things you want to, or that money is easy to make. Why not? Just because Mom and Dad argued about money doesn't make it accurate that money is hard to make. That was just something you decided in a moment when you were five!

You really can make a different choice. You randomly came to a conclusion the first time you gave meaning to a particular experience, so why can't you draw a different conclusion now?

Given you have the choice, the free will, to choose what something means, wouldn't you opt for something empowering that makes you feel good?

FUNDAMENTALS

- Your subconscious mind determines the level of success in all areas of your life. We do not create what we want, we create what we believe.

- When you set a goal or intention, you indicate to your brain that anything associated with it is important, and your brain goes to work bringing to your attention information and opportunities to help you get there.

- Whatever you are trying to build or create, it must have a firm footing. Work on the foundation first – your beliefs.

- Limiting beliefs are simply a series of neuro-synaptic connections in your brain that represent your memory of something and the meaning you gave that experience. They aren't facts, merely choices that you've made over and over again.

- Think of your beliefs as a story. If you improve the content of the story you tell every day about yourself and your life, you will start to believe, and your life will become ever improving.

EXERCISES

1. Uninstall and reinstall

In this exercise, I want you to write down your response to a series of questions. Just write down what comes to mind immediately. Don't worry about neatness or spelling or grammar. Just write freely and let the words flow. The idea is to take an inventory of the things that are consciously, or unconsciously, holding you back.

These questions are designed to make you think and to identify limiting beliefs you perhaps didn't even know you had.

For anything you identify, you don't need to "fix" it. Begin by realizing that beliefs are nothing more than programming you have developed from the influential people and experiences in your life. Here goes...

- *What are the current obstacles that might be preventing you from living the life of your dreams?*

- *What would you have to know to take a baby step toward living that life?*

- *What would you need to think about yourself to be successful in that life?*

- *What would you have to trust about how others would support you in making your dream a reality?*

- *What are you clinging to that's preventing you from seeing your potential clearly?*

- *Can you accept that your path in life may need to unfold as you progress?*

- *Are you holding on to negative emotions because they fill a void in your life?*

- *Are you refusing to let go because you're trying to punish someone?*

- *If a clear, guaranteed path for living your dream was laid out in front of you, what would be the first step?*

- *Are you refusing to let go of the past because you're punishing yourself?*

I expect that the output from these questions highlighted some limiting beliefs. I have been through this process, and I found it challenging. I highlighted some fears pretty clearly, and I highlighted some behaviors that were because of those fears. However, it was challenging to connect some of my fears and unwanted behavior with the limiting beliefs that were causing them. Take a while with this. It's okay. It might take some time.

Let me give you an example of how I went through the process and what I uncovered about the old me:

- It jumped out at me that one of the things preventing me from living the life of my dreams was the need for other people's permission and acceptance. If I wanted something different, then I would have to make changes, and it would impact those around me.

- I definitely felt like I couldn't make a change or, God forbid, take a risk without adversely affecting those closest to me.

- Then I asked myself why it mattered what other people thought. Not selfishly or indulgently, just acknowledging that it's my life and I am free to live it the way I want.

- The answer that came back was that I didn't want to risk not being accepted. I also felt like I needed permission to make a change.

- Then the bombshell: what was a really afraid of? I was scared of losing people. I was worried that if I changed, I would lose those around me.

- It gets worse: why would I lose them? Well, because I would be following my heart and making a change for me. I realized I was not 100% me, ever. Mostly me, of course, but in every relationship, in every area of my life, I was holding back a bit of me. I was replacing that part with a little of what I thought others wanted and expected.

Do you want to know the disempowering belief beneath it all?

People will leave me if I show them who I really am.

Don't ask me where this came from and don't ask me why I adopted that belief – that could be the subject of a whole other book! I'm sure we could point to all manner of childhood events or more recent circumstances.

What matters is that I identified this disempowering belief – the corrupt program file, if you will – and I uninstalled it. I uninstalled it merely by bringing it to light and seeing it for what it was: bullshit! A disempowering belief that was causing me to hold back and be inauthentic.

Do you want to know what I installed in its place?

People love me *because* of who I am.

Now, that's better. That's a supportive belief. That fuels me to be authentic and genuine.

Back to you. How is your analysis coming along?

Assuming you have identified one or more limiting beliefs that have been holding you back, I want you to understand something fundamental: beliefs are neither right nor wrong, they are simply beliefs. Therefore, you can change them if you wish. If a theory is not helping you, replace it with one that does. Instead of being limited by doubt or uncertainty, you can be fueled by confidence and positivity.

So, let's install some new beliefs. Shaping your reality in new ways requires believing new things.

What you've believed so far has brought you to where you are today, right? Then moving toward a different life requires different beliefs. Below is a list of the views and ways of thinking that have helped me to transform my life. Go through the list twice. During your first read, certain things will jump off the page at you. Circle or highlight them. In the next pass, mark the *ten* that resonate with you the most.

> *I think "both" rather than "either/or."*
> *I am young and wildly successful.*
> *I act in spite of fear.*
> *I focus on what I want, not what I don't want.*
> *I am willing to do whatever it takes.*

I am so much bigger than my problems.
I never give up.
I trust myself.
I believe in myself.
If they can do it, I can do it.
I am a good receiver.
I am creating riches to share with the world.
I add value to the world.
I can handle any challenge which arises.
I can do anything.
I never blame, justify, or complain.
I love my life.
I create my life.
I am a leader.
I am a force for good.
I complete what I start.
I live with passion.
I take massive action.
I think BIG.
I get paid based on the value I provide.
I am a money magnet.
I am outstanding at managing my money.
I am comfortable being with discomfort.
There are no problems, only opportunities to grow.
I focus on contributing to others.
My body is magnificent.
I feel incredible.
I am powerful beyond measure.
I am unshakeable.
I don't 'have to,' I choose to.
I live in integrity.
I approve of myself.
I don't have to please everyone.

I don't take anything personally.
I ask for help and support.
I take one step at a time.
I ask how I am creating this situation.
I speak with compassion.
I forgive myself and others easily.

Make changes to them, enhance them, and personalize them. Make them your own. Then write down your ten beliefs in a personal journal or notebook that you will keep with you.

You can begin to adopt these new beliefs immediately by saying them out loud, declaring them to the world. Do this for at least the next ten days and see how you feel.

The following is another real-life example. This limiting belief actually came from someone close to me.

I used to dress really smart all the time. That's no bad thing, by the way, but the reason was less than ideal. I had no idea this was relevant for me until it was brought to my attention. I was dressing smart and a little older than my age because I believed, deep down, that you had to be of a certain age and to demonstrate a certain maturity to be successful in business. I grew up believing that successful businessmen wore suits and ties all the time, and that was a sign of success; of wealth.

Well, it might be, but look at the tech millionaires and billionaires who rock up to work in scruffy T-shirts and ripped jeans. Who said you had to wear a suit and tie to be important and/or successful?

Since I made this realization, I have been dressing younger – skinny jeans, smart sneakers and nice T-shirts. You know what, it's a damn sight more comfortable and I feel great! Not long after the change, a close friend of mine actually said, "Wow, you look great – so much younger." Funny, right?

Don't get me wrong, there is a time and place for dressing smart. I still take pride in my tailor-made suits and Italian silk ties. I just don't *need* to wear them to feel important or successful anymore. I wear them with pleasure when the occasion is right. I don't need a uniform anymore; I dress like me.

This ties in perfectly with one of my favorite power phrases that I made up for myself, and I say every day, "I am a young and wildly successful entrepreneur and business owner." The entrepreneur and business owner references are obvious: creativity, freedom, and autonomy. I want to highlight the "young" part. It's important to me to think young because I was looking and acting older than my age for some time, to seek my old definition of success. Every time I think of being young *and* successful at the same time, I get goosebumps and feel pumped. Especially now I believe that I'm actually getting more youthful because of it, and that's amazing!

Summary instructions

1. Write down your response to the questions. Don't worry about neatness or spelling or grammar. Just write freely and let it flow.

2. Realize that beliefs are nothing more than programming you have developed from the influential people and experiences in your life.

3. Read the list of empowering beliefs twice. On the second pass, mark the **ten** that resonate with you the most.

4. Make them your own. Then write down your **ten** beliefs in a personal journal or notebook that you will keep with you.

5. Say your new beliefs out loud every day for at least **ten** days and see how you feel.

TOOL #3: PRESENCE

———•———

"Be present – it is the only moment that matters."

– Peaceful Warrior

TOOL #3: PRESENCE

---

pres · ence

noun

the state or fact of existing, occurring or being present in a place or thing.

Let's think about dogs for a minute. I happen to believe that dogs are magical. Well, they are lovely, at least. I have the most incredibly precious long-haired dachshund. My dog is handsome, cute, funny, loving, loyal, and I love my dog so much it hurts. I mean, seriously. When he gives me the puppy-dog eyes and lifts his paw because he wants something, my heart physically aches. Or when he comes bounding across the room towards me carrying one of his chew toys that's bigger than he is, I melt into the floor.

He helped enormously with my anxiety and worry when he came into my life. I thought he had somehow "absorbed" my anxiety and worry. One day I realized that was not entirely accurate.

Dogs are totally present. I mean, I can hide one of his toys when he gets carried away and starts eating the stuffing. He looks at me with those sad puppy-dog eyes, then I'll tickle his ears, and he's smiling again like nothing ever happened. My dog lives in the moment.

Here's the thing, when I'm with him, I am present too. He puts me in a state of here and now where there is no fear, no anxiety, and no worry. So, he doesn't *absorb* my anxiety and worry, he brings me into the moment where my anxiety and worry *evaporate*.

Somehow, dogs know that all is well. Somehow, they understand the power of *now*. They don't worry or fret or make laws or rules or try to control. They simply live for now.

When you're with them, there's nothing but love, nothing but being present and grounded. No thoughts of work tomorrow, the business trip next week, or the project deadline at the end of the month. Just you and them, right here, right now.

Can one really eliminate anxiety and worry merely by being present? Absolutely, yes.

WHAT IS ANXIETY?

I used to suffer terribly from anxiety. It was a regular occurrence for me that something "serious" happened at work or the receipt of a troublesome email would trigger severe feelings of anxiety. For me, it feels like a surge of adrenaline shocking my entire body, and a physical reaction like butterflies or a sick feeling in the pit of my stomach.

I knew it wasn't right, and I knew it was an extreme reaction. But I had no idea how to avoid it. Nor did I have any idea what was going on in my mind. I chalked it up to life in the corporate world, and I simply got better at calming myself down after the fact. I would try to put things in perspective or compose myself by making a cup of tea or coffee. It was a regular occurrence for me and, at times, debilitating.

It wasn't until someone explained to me the power of presence that I learned how to control and, ultimately, eliminate anxiety and worry. You don't feel anxious or worried when you are present. In the present moment, there is nothing other than bliss, joy and happiness.

Now it's my turn to help you: to me, anxiety is merely living in the future. Fear, anxiety, worry are all related to the anticipation of pain – they are all projecting into the future; an experience of unease about an event that hasn't happened, or some uncertainty.

Think about it, that feeling of panic before a big meeting you're underprepared for, or the feeling of nervousness when you don't know how someone will react to the news you have to share, or the feeling of anxiety when you're running out of time to get something important completed. This is *projection*. You are projecting into the future and thinking about an adverse outcome.

Worry is basically using your imagination to dwell upon something you don't want. So, the trick is to focus on the moment, the here and now, and the feelings of anxiety and worry will disappear. The future doesn't exist, so you have nothing to be anxious about. When you're in the moment, you experience an incredible feeling of bliss and joy – the belief that everything is just fine. It's wonderful being able to focus on what you're doing and enjoy it.

CALM AMONGST THE CHAOS

You can probably identify with the fact that sometimes your day seems to spiral out of control and descend into utter chaos. I've been there more times than I choose to count. You may wonder how it's possible to be calm in the middle of all that chaos and madness? The answer is simple, though not always easy to put into practice: *learn to be present.*

No matter how out of control your day may seem, no matter how stressful your job or life becomes, the act of being present can become an oasis. It can change your life and it's incredibly simple.

When you ask people what things stop them from having a calm and peaceful day, responses may include:

- Too many things coming at once.

- Seemingly unnecessary interruptions.

- Obvious lack of control.

- Not knowing what to do.

- A confrontation between colleagues.

The anxiety and worry that results from any of these factors can be solved by one thing: being present.

When you look at the list of factors, you will see that they are entirely in the mind. I acknowledge there are events and circumstances at work which cannot be ignored: an overflowing email inbox, an uncontrollable task, interruptions, and distractions. But it's how our mind handles those external forces that is the problem.

If you are completely present, the events and circumstances are no longer a problem, because there is only you and that external force in the moment. There is nothing else you need to worry about.

If your colleague interrupts you, you may stress out because you have other things to worry about and someone else is adding to your worries or disrupting your flow. Alternatively, you can simply be present, and then there is only you and your colleague. You can appreciate them for who they are, listen to them, and be grateful you have this moment. All the while, you are present in that moment with your colleague your unread emails, the backlog of voicemails, and the stack of review papers do not exist. When you're done talking with your colleague, you can move back to what you were doing before.

If your boss demands that you deal with an urgent task, you can stress out because you have so many other things you need to do and not enough time. Alternatively, you can be present and focus intently on that task, and then there is only that one task and you. When you have completed the urgent task, you can tackle the next item on your list.

Being present is a way to handle any problem, any distraction, any potential stressor. It allows everything else to fade away, leaving only you and whatever you're dealing with right now.

PRACTICE, PRACTICE, PRACTICE

The method for being present is relatively simple. Most people don't learn to be present because they don't practice being present, not because it's hard to do.

When you practice something regularly, you become good at it. It becomes more a mode of being than a task on your to-do list. Practice it and being present will become natural.

Here's how to do it: whatever you're doing, focus entirely on doing that one thing. Pay attention to every aspect of what you're doing – the size, shape and color of what you're looking at, how your body feels, any sensations you experience, what thoughts you can hear.

You will notice your thoughts jump to other things. That's okay – you are not attempting to force all other thoughts from your mind. By becoming aware of your thoughts bouncing around, you have identified the self-awareness needed to bring yourself back to your present task. Just notice your thoughts jumping around and gently bring yourself back to the task at hand.

Do this once, and then do it again. Don't worry about how many times you must do it.

If you're not used to this, it may become tiring at first. Don't worry about that. Let yourself rest if you grow tired of the exercise. Come back to it a little later and practice again. It's not meant to be exhausting. Instead, you should notice how your worries melt away when you come into the moment, and you enjoy your present task much more.

Practice throughout your day, every day. It works really well to come up with one or more reminders to be present. For example, your child's voice, your co-workers appearing before you, a regular event on your computer, the noise of traffic. Anything that can serve as a friendly reminder to bring yourself back into the present moment.

Practice, repeatedly, in small, manageable steps. Each exercise helps you to find some peace and calm in the middle of your busy day.

PRESENT MOMENT AWARENESS

Let's take this concept a little further and talk about *present moment awareness*.

We can all think of an event or situation that has triggered us to respond negatively – whether that is feeling anger, showing frustration, or experiencing disappointment. But when you stop and think purely about the event or situation itself, there's actually nothing there; it means nothing. When you think about it, nothing is anything until we make it something; until we layer it with meaning.

For example, I recall a morning when I was working from home. My calendar was back to back with tasks, calls and other commitments. Included on the list of obligations were receiving a furniture delivery and taking my dog for a groom. I came up with the idea of working from my favorite coffee shop in town during the two to three hours that my dog was being groomed. This idea started to get me really excited when I decided that I would treat myself to a flat white from the coffee shop – their coffee is in my top five favorites of all time!

Guess what happened. The furniture delivery company showed up unannounced when I was taking a shower before leaving the house for the groomers. My mind raced off at 100mph, thinking through all the permutations and combinations of how I could make this work.

The only solution was to get dressed quickly, welcome the delivery guys, leave immediately to drop off my dog at the groomers while they unloaded the truck, then return home to be here while the delivery guys did what they needed to do.

Then it hit me: I wasn't going to be able to relax in my favorite coffee shop after all, and I wasn't going to get that coffee I'd been dreaming about all morning!

And then the rant:

- This is bullshit! I don't ask for much. Why do people have to inconvenience me all the time?

- I'm never going to be able to get my dog to the groomers on time because I'm going to have to deal with the delivery guys.

- These damn delivery companies never show up at the right time – they should have called or texted me in advance like they said they would!

So on and so forth. You know the drill.

I am pleased to report that this process lasted only a second or two before I caught myself and snapped back immediately.

The point here is that the entire negative experience, albeit brief for me, was made up. The event, in this case, was merely a furniture delivery company arriving at my home. What's the big deal? It's nothing, it's a big fat zero, it literally has no meaning. All the other shit was layered on by me and my mind. The entire negative experience was down to me and my mind projecting potential outcomes and drawing unwanted conclusions.

Think of it like a bowl of vanilla ice cream. It's neither good nor bad; it's just vanilla ice cream. That represents an event or situation in its present form. Then we pour shit all over the top of ice cream, we eat it, and we complain that it tastes like shit. Well, it tastes like shit because you covered it in shit before you ate it, dum dum!

ACCEPTING WHAT IS

The key to achieving freedom from these negative experiences is accepting "what is." I don't mean being a pushover and never taking action to improve your life. Quite the opposite. I mean acknowledging present moment events and situations in your life for what they are – just moments – so that you remain in command of your mind and feel empowered to choose how you respond.

It is never what actually happens that causes us to have a bad experience, it is what we add to what happens by the meaning we attribute to it, and the narrative we feed to ourselves. The latter is what truly impacts our life.

You have a choice to resist "what is" and make it feel bad, or accept it and move on with your life. Basically, you have the choice of whether to add the shit or not. That is the power of present moment awareness.

Accepting what is becomes much easier when you learn to separate the reality of an event or situation from all the stories you tell.

Think of it as truth versus narrative.

When something happens, and you start to feel tension or resistance building up inside you, ask yourself immediately what is true about the situation. You know that you are projecting and storytelling, otherwise you wouldn't be feeling bad. Asking yourself what is true about the situation identifies the "what is." All the rest, which is making you feel bad, is "thoughts about what is."

Practice separating the two as a way to bring yourself into the present and allow your feelings to pass. I'm not suggesting that you will (or should) ever get to the point that you are a feeling-less creative. Not at all; you must feel what you're feeling, that's a massive part of life. What I am suggesting is that present moment awareness and accepting what is allows any associated bad feelings to pass more quickly.

Look at it this way: we aren't living in reality at all because 99% of what we experience is made up in our heads. Having this awareness and the ability to separate what is from your thoughts about what is, enables you to live consciously. This means acting from choice in the present moment rather than acting out of habit from the past. Doesn't that sound like a more blissful way to live?

LIVING BLISSFULLY

One of the best methods to deal with serious challenges is to put yourself in the present moment as much as possible. We tend to worry about things that haven't happened yet or fixate on stuff from the past. If we are entirely in the present moment, then there is no future or past to worry about.

The secret to a blissful life is actually enjoying the passage of time. That is profound, given that we are living in a society completely obsessed with the all-powerful causative past and the all-absorbing importance of the future. We don't live in the present moment because it generally feels like nothing more than an infinitesimally short time. Most of us have no present. Our consciousness is almost completely preoccupied with memory and expectation, busy replaying the past and rehearsing the future.

The only way to enjoy the passage of time is to exist in the now. It means being in the here and now, not in the future with imagined fear or in the past with remembered guilt.

Life is right now; it is not later. Be present when you're with your loved ones, enjoy everything that you are right now, and appreciate what is right in front of you. The future hasn't happened yet, so enjoy this very moment; every moment.

Live in the moment and you will enjoy freedom from fear and worry. Don't just take my word for it, try it and see for yourself.

FUNDAMENTALS

- You do not feel anxious or worried when you are present. In the present moment, there is nothing other than bliss, joy and happiness.

- Fear, anxiety, and worry are all related to the anticipation of pain – they are projecting into the future and cause us to experience unease about an event that hasn't happened yet or something with uncertainty.

- No matter how out of control your day may seem, no matter how stressful your job or life becomes, the act of being present can create an oasis.

- The method for being present is relatively simple: whatever you are doing, focus entirely on doing that one thing. Pay attention to every aspect of what you are doing. You should notice how your worries melt away and you enjoy your present task much more.

- It is never what actually happens that causes us to have a bad experience, it is what we add to those things in terms of meaning and narrative. The latter is what impacts our lives.

- Presence means being in the here and now, not in the future with imagined fear or in the past with remembered guilt.

EXERCISES

1. Here and now

If you feel anxious or worried, ask yourself these two questions and say these two responses, one after the other:

> *Where am I?*
> "Here."
> *What time is it?*
> "Now."

Relax into it, and *really* say "here" and "now" in response to the questions. Pause in between each question and answer. Let yourself come into the present moment. Feelings of anxiety and worry will dissipate.

Sometimes, when I was really worked up about something, it would take a few rounds of "here and now" to eliminate the anxiety. The results were amazing. I felt the anxiety and worry leave my body, my arms and legs relaxed. I felt grounded and calm.

Try it and see for yourself.

Summary instructions

1. When you feel anxious or worried, ask yourself these two questions:

   Where am I?
   What time is it?

2. Relax into it and say the following responses:

   "Here."
   "Now."

3. Pause in-between each question and answer.

4. Let yourself come into the present moment and notice the feelings of anxiety and worry dissipate.

5. Repeat as often as necessary to eliminate the feeling of anxiety and worry.

TOOL #4: DISSOCIATION

"If there is no enemy within, the enemy outside can do us no harm."

– African Proverb

TOOL #4: DISSOCIATION

---

dis · so · ci · a · tion

noun

the disconnection or separation of something from something else or the state of being disconnected.

I was at lunch with a friend of mine. We used to work together. We were sat having a lovely chat about the future of her career. At that point, she was two or three years away from making partner at her firm. She was entering the partner pipeline process. She loved what she did, and she was really good at it. She was okay with the seemingly unreasonable pressure, the stress, the time demands, and the typical corporate hustle. It seemed to motivate her – to drive her forward. She found significant meaning in what she did for a living, which translated into her being emotionally invested in her role and delivering work of the highest standard.

I was sat there feeling genuinely pleased for her. I was proud of her, even. I could see that this was what she wanted, and I knew she deserved it. It was going to be the start of the next phase of her career with incredible challenges and lucrative rewards.

Then I started to think about when I made the decision not to go down that route. It was a bold move on my part. For the longest time, I was Mr Corporate America. The turning point in my life was when I decided I was going to start my own company. It was a radical change in direction. It brought more risk with the lack of stability, but it brought the opportunity for considerably more satisfaction and fulfillment for me. I was starting the process of building something of my own, and this was in stark contrast to what I'd pursued for so many years before.

Once upon a time, I would have been envious of my friend, even jealous. It wasn't that long ago that I thought being admitted to the partnership at a large organization was the ultimate measure of success and achievement. My identity used to be rooted in what I did for a living and the rate of my career progression. So, a friend of mine making partner before me would have hurt a little bit. Not now. I sat there feeling joy and happiness for my friend. My heart glowed at what this meant to her, and what an incredible achievement this would be. *Good for her*, I was thinking.

Then I started to think about other friends who were approaching partner promotion at their firm; working hard to take that big step and take their career to the next level. I was filled with similar feelings of pride and appreciation for my friends. *Good for them*, I was thinking.

Then, out of nowhere, a voice in my head said, "How are you going to feel two years from now when you've fucked everything up, and all your friends are partners and you're not?"

Wow. What a terrible thing to say! How upsetting and rude. Who said that? What a jerk!

This story highlights the realization that we all have a voice in our heads – an internal narrator who continually has us wanting stuff, rejecting stuff, judging people, comparing ourselves to people, and engaging in ruthless self-criticism.

How would you feel if someone talked to you like that for real? How would you respond to a person who said something vile like that? After a short period and only a few incidents, I'm sure they would no longer be part of your life.

Somehow, when your inner voice says things like that, you don't tell it to leave. No matter how much pain or trouble it causes, you listen. It's time to change that. Let's dig deeper into who's saying what and think about who's really in control.

This is a "big one". Seriously, I mean it. A happy and fulfilling life is rooted in taking command of your mind. The biggest obstacle you'll ever have to overcome is your mind. If you can overcome that, you can overcome anything.

YOU ARE NOT THE VOICE INSIDE YOUR HEAD

Have you ever noticed the internal dialogue going on inside your head?

If right now you hear, "What is he talking about. There's no voice in my head!" – that's the voice I'm talking about!

If you spend time observing this mind chatter, the first thing you will notice is that it never shuts up. It just keeps going and going. When left unattended, it just talks.

What kind of mind chatter do you experience? Does your mind do a little complaining, questioning, or mostly worrying? What does your mind say?

I'm willing to bet that your mind chatter says very little to empower you or prepare you for challenges. In fact, I'm sure that your mind chatter is not supportive at all. Your mind chatter is pretty much entirely negative. Am I right?

So, who is this non-supportive *being* that's saying these nasty things in your head?

It's obviously you, so really the question is: if it's you, then who's the one listening? Well, that's you too.

If that's you as well, then it seems like there might be two of you. Right? Of course, there are!

One of the most important things to understand is the difference between your true self and your false self and how the two "yous" fight for control.

Your true, or higher, self is in stark contrast to what we will call your *false self* or *conditioned mind*.

The conflict between your higher self and the false self is universal. If you pay close attention, you can actually see how the two "yous" are arguing. For example, when someone gets angry with themselves, their higher self and their false self are sparring with one another. Or when someone asks, "Why did I let myself eat that slice of chocolate cake?" the answer is because your false self (or lower-level you) won out over the more thoughtful, higher-level you.

Once you understand how your logical/conscious part and your emotional/subconscious part are in conflict with each other, you can begin to master your mind.

CONDITIONING

Your true self is your original self – the person you came into the world as. Your false self is the person you've learned to be. We all arrive as an empty vessel and we fill up over time with what we learn, and how we become conditioned by our experiences.

We start out open, spontaneous, accepting, peaceful and joyous. Then we learn how to survive in this world.

This comes from our personal experiences, starting from when we were just babies. Think about when we are taken home for the first time as a baby and when we experience the feeling of hunger for the first time. We feel uncomfortable, we're not sure what to do, so we "coo" and "goo" for a while but nothing happens.

Then we get hungrier and even more uncomfortable, so we try a little whimper. Still, nothing happens for us.

Finally, we get desperate and have to take drastic action, so we let out a big, bellowing scream!

Mom and/or Dad come running in, they pick us up, and they give us all the attention and food we want. Excellent result. We make a mental note in our *manual of life* that the louder we cry, the faster they come running. I bet you know at least one person who is still using the same strategy years later as an adult!

This conditioning becomes our way of being and governs how we think and how we behave in this world. It's a construct by which we determine who we're supposed to be, how we think we're supposed to act – all made up by us when we were young to get what we wanted.

Consequently, our thoughts are generally more defensive and/or fear based. Critically, because our way of being is based on our need to *survive*, not *thrive*.

We learned, or created, a way of being which is our personality and is merely a collection of ideas, experiences, and programmed responses. We'll call this our ego self.

Our way of being is generally based on what we learned as a child. We learned a lot on our own, and we were conditioned by everything around us – parents, teachers, media outlets, family, friends, TV, etc.

I like to think of my ego self as my personal bodyguard. He's like the lookout guy who yells at the top of his lungs anytime there's the slightest threat: "Iceberg, right ahead!"

He's just doing his job. Often times it's a good job he's there because his warnings are helpful for me to quickly correct course and avoid an incident.

But the point is, *he's not me*. I am the captain of the ship. He is there to inform me. I appreciate him and I'm glad he's there. I also acknowledge that he is excellent at his job – based on the frequency and volume of warnings that come my way!

I understand that I have a choice. I don't have to listen to my mind. I take the warning on board, I process it, I assess the situation for myself, and I take appropriate action.

YOUR THOUGHTS ARE NOT YOUR THOUGHTS

The thinking that is continuously taking place in our heads is part of our survival mechanism. Our brains are always trying to interpret what's happening, moment by moment, and throwing out opinions about everything – other people, money, the economy, everything – in the form of thoughts.

Our brains are a meaning-making machine. It's a mechanism that helps our young, impressionable minds make sense of the world around us. We are looking to attach meaning to everything we experience. We are always being programmed by our experiences and the resultant impact and consequences.

Now, here's the problem: we carry these meanings with us into adulthood. You need to recognize that all of this stuff, this "personality" conditioning, programming, way of being, is not the real you. It's a recording of information that you learned which is continuing to play unconsciously and directing your thoughts and actions automatically.

I want you to realize that you are not the recording. You are not even the record. You are the one playing the recording; you are the record player.

In other words, you are not your mind. Your mind is a part of you, and you are much bigger and much greater than it. You are what holds your mind. It's a part of you, just like you'd refer to "my hand" or "my foot."

Dissociation from your thoughts in this way gives you enormous power.

BIOLOGY OF THE MIND

The concept of "dissociation" fits precisely with contemporary neuroscience that identifies a particular part of the brain as the source of the familiar internal narrative that gives us our sense of self.

Neuroscientists have characterized the quirky, undependable quality of the tale told by the mind. Some have said that the left cerebral hemisphere of humans is prone to fabricating oral narratives that do not necessarily accord with the truth.

Others have noted that the left brain weaves its story to convince itself, and you, that it is in full control.

Basically, we have what amounts to a spin-doctor in the left brain!

Solid experimental work shows that we tend to believe our own stories. Even when we think we're rational, our own false thinking convinces us.

Don't underestimate the significance of how your thoughts impact the way you feel and subsequently behave. We are the only beings that can think a thought and become angry; think a thought and become playful; think a thought and be worried; think a thought and feel love.

The best way to tackle the never-ending mind chatter is to step back and view it objectively. I don't think many people know or understand this. They fall into the trap of believing that their conditioning is who they really are, so they are on autopilot, run continuously by their false self.

Once we separate ourselves from these patterns of thinking, we can actually start to question whether or not we even agree with these thoughts. Self-awareness and challenging the mind is a way out of its self-made trap.

You can choose to let the commentary know you hear it, then move on. You don't have to engage in conversation.

GET OUT OF YOUR HEAD

When you get inside your head, it means you're believing the most limiting thoughts that your mind brings to your attention. We all have a two-million-year-old brain which is not designed to make us happy; it is designed for survival. It's always looking for what's wrong.

There is a specific part of the brain responsible for this: the amygdala; the body's alarm system. A small mass of gray matter inside each cerebral hemisphere, the amygdala is responsible for emotions, survival instincts and memory. In other words, the brain area associated with figuring out whether external stimuli is a threat.

The amygdala is the reason we feel afraid. It controls the way we react to certain stimuli or events we see as potentially threatening or dangerous.

When you hear a noise at night, your "old" brain makes a split-second decision whether it's a threat. The outcome of that decision can then trigger a series of nervous and physical responses. Faster than your conscious mind can think, that bump in the night activates the fight-or-flight response. Your heart beats faster to pump blood to your muscles, the hair on your body stands up to make you look more substantial, you begin to sweat and breathe more rapidly.

For our ancient ancestors, this response enabled them to perceive and react to threats faster and survive. It was absolutely critical and often the difference between living to see another day and meeting your end. We have inherited this highly attuned survival mechanism.

FEAR IS NATURAL, YOUR RESPONSE IS NOT

Fear is a response to a perceived threat; it is automatic and is programmed into each of us through millions of years of evolution.

94

The trouble is, we don't stop to think about the fact that our response is based on perception. It's pretty helpful when you're a caveman and a saber-toothed tiger jumps out on you. I would be extremely grateful for the immediate warning and extreme reaction to this genuine threat to my safety. In this case, I'm good with the rapid increase in heart rate and the surge of adrenaline coursing through my veins.

But when you realize that you've forgotten to do something at work or your boss asks you to come into their office because they want to "talk", are you really in mortal danger? Should you experience the same feelings of panic? Should you have such a severe reaction? No, of course not. We simply have not learned how to adapt our highly attuned survival mechanism to our modern environment.

We think this way of being is natural. I would say it's *normal* for most people in the working world, but it's anything but *natural*.

RECONDITIONING YOUR MIND

The mind talks all the time because you gave it a job to do – you use it as a protection mechanism. This makes you feel more secure. As long as that's what you want, you will be forced to use your mind to buffer you from life, instead of actually living it.

You can recondition your mind, slowly recording over the old tapes with newer, more supportive beliefs and habits for yourself. Or you can bypass the entire fear-based, problem-based system and live from your higher or true self. You are the real captain of the ship.

Personally, I take great satisfaction from seeing my higher self and my ego self as separate and distinct. Frankly, my ego self is a brat most of the time! He's whiney, he complains, and he's always worried about what other people think of him.

Don't get me wrong, I love my ego self. He is part of me and I appreciate the constant feedback and warnings when it comes to taking on new challenges. I just choose not to let these fear-based thoughts hold me back.

My higher self, on the other hand, is a giant of a man. He is calm and measured. He has a powerful presence and peace about him. He always knows what to do, and he acts with integrity and compassion. Interestingly, for me, he doesn't speak. Communication comes in the form of feelings and more a sense of "knowing" what to do. I often visualize or see a "look" from him when I doubt myself or move to take a step in the wrong direction. It's almost like having an influential parent who can make you feel loved and supported or let you know you're doing something wrong with just a look.

Your false self and your true self are always there with you. The key is to disassociate from your conditioned mind and the fear-based thoughts that come along with it. This offers you the opportunity to choose what to believe and how to act, which is so much more empowering.

You can choose to observe your thoughts separately from yourself and determine whether to listen and act on them, especially when they're not supportive. I like to think of it as clouds that pass by in the sky. They're there, and you can see them, but you don't have to pay attention to them.

You access your true self as soon as you quieten your conditioned mind; as soon as you clear the mind chatter. If you can quiet your mind, your true self is available. You don't have to do anything or go anywhere.

The key is to be aware of the separation between you and your ego self. It makes such a difference to your day-to-day life when you know that the scary, fearful thoughts popping into your head are not actually real. They are just thoughts. They are only warnings from your defense mechanism.

This leads to the quieting of your mind – and with a quiet mind, you will naturally be peaceful, powerful, joyous, and tap into your inner wisdom.

If you disassociate from your thoughts, you will experience incredible power, like you are taking back command of the ship. And, frankly, you are.

The only truly scary thing is fear itself.

FUNDAMENTALS

- A happy and fulfilling life is rooted in taking command of your mind. If you can overcome that, you can overcome anything.

- The thinking that is continuously taking place in our heads is part of our ancient survival mechanism. Our brains are meaning-making machines, always trying to interpret what's happening and throwing out opinions about everything in the form of thoughts.

- The best way to tackle this never-ending mind chatter is to step back and view it objectively. You can choose to observe your thoughts separately from yourself and determine whether or not to listen and act on them.

- You are not your mind; your mind is a part of you, and you are much bigger and much greater than your mind.

- Dissociation from your thoughts gives you enormous power.

EXERCISES

1. Internal dialogue

When I approach something new, like everyone else, I feel a degree of fear or nervousness. The more aware I become of my mind playing tricks on me, the more I see that my mind is always finding new ways, new excuses, and new fears to try to stop me moving forward. We all have an internal board of directors in our head – and the Chairman of the board is fear!

Explore the chatter your mind throws at you to stop you in your tracks. Now that you know all these disempowering thoughts are not really *you*, you can start to identify how your mind tries to scare you into submission.

I'll give you a few examples of how mine tries to stop me. See if you can identify with any of these:

> *You can't do that, you don't have the relevant experience.*
> *What if you're wrong? It's not worth the risk!*
> *You will look stupid and people will think less of you.*
> *You have responsibilities, so you should play it safe.*
> *You don't have what it takes so leave it to others who do.*
> *It's a gamble, you won't succeed so don't even try.*
> *How would you feel if this goes wrong?*
> *Just wait for a while and see if you still want to do it.*
> *Maybe next year, I think you're okay for now.*
> *A lot is going on, so it's a bad idea to do anything else.*
> *The worst thing you could do is rush into anything new.*

Now make a list of at least ten examples of how your mind tries to stop you. Look out for how these and others come up as you go forward.

One more thing: even now, knowing what I know, I sometimes find it hard to immediately tell whether the thought in my head is *me* or my *mind*. Because an idea or an impulse not to do something could be fear talking, or it could be sound reasoning.

In other words, if I have a feeling that I don't want to do something, I generally know it's my mind trying to stop me. But what if I actually *shouldn't* do it and it's *me* trying to stop me because it's not actually the right way to go?!

I think the answer is that it's all about power. If your thoughts about a particular course of action are empowering, then it's probably the right answer. If your thinking on a specific course of action is disempowering, then it's probably not the right answer.

Here's a real-life example to illustrate the point.

I was once given the opportunity to invest in some real estate. The magnitude of the deal was much larger than I was used to, so I was, understandably, uncomfortable. I really didn't want to do it because I would be financially overstretched. Now, doesn't that sound like I'm a wuss? Doesn't that sound like I found an excuse not to move forward just because I was scared?

Well, yes and no. The concern over being financially overstretched was real. But that was not the reason I had doubts about the deal. I checked my emotions at the door and I looked at the metrics of the transaction again. The numbers didn't make financial sense. I was pushing myself to make this one happen because I wanted to invest. There was considerable uncertainty over the income, and the return wasn't there.

So, walking away from the deal was not a wimpy, disempowering decision. It was a well thought-out, empowering decision. The investment did not work for me.

Had I done my due diligence and the numbers made sense, then not going through with the deal would have meant giving in to my disempowering thoughts and beliefs. Do you see the difference?

Summary instructions

1. Read the examples of how your mind tries to stop you and see how may of them you identify with.

2. Write a list of at least **ten** examples of how your mind works to prevent you.

3. Look out for how your examples (and others) come up for you going forward.

4. When you're struggling to determine a course of action because you can't tell if it's you or your mind, think about which way is more empowering.

TOOL #5: INTEGRITY

——◆——

"Integrity is the seed for achievement.
It is the principle that never fails."

– Earl Nightingale

TOOL #5: INTEGRITY

———•———

in · teg · ri · ty

noun

1. the quality of being honest and having strong moral principles; moral uprightness.

2. the state of being whole and undivided.

At the time of writing this chapter of the book, I have a craft coffee brand (**www.cupoffee.com**) that is only a few months old. I decided with my friend and business partner that we would start an online retail store. We wanted to learn from the setup process, take on a side project together, and create another source of passive income.

We both love coffee – the whole process: selecting our choice of freshly roasted coffee, grinding the beans, brewing the coffee, then enjoying the fruits of our labor – and we frequently catch up over coffee. Our conversation is always riveting, but the coffee may be lackluster. It became clear that creating a craft coffee brand was the answer.

It was an enjoyable process. We did everything from start to finish: building the website, branding, sourcing the beans, establishing supplier contacts, figuring out distribution, putting payment processing in place, etc. This is a significant business venture about which we are both excited and proud.

But do you know what the best part is for me? It's not necessarily working together on the next steps or having operational discussions, or making plans to take the business to the next level and reach more people. The best part for me is the fact that we said we would do it and we did it.

Without knowing how, the steps involved, or what was needed, we made it happen. We made a commitment and we followed through on it. That is power.

WHAT IS INTEGRITY?

Integrity essentially means something that is whole and complete. In other words, it's doing what you say you are going to do and finishing what you start, consistently. If you do those things, then you have the best possible chance of being successful and fulfilled in whatever area you choose to pursue.

Have you ever had someone tell you that you're all talk? Or that you talk a good game? If yes, then you'll know that hurts!

It's not okay that you don't stick to your commitments or keep your word. Integrity is the most essential characteristic to creating real success in life. If you don't have it, you're never going to take your life to the next level.

It's not okay that you're late. It's not okay that you break promises. If you don't keep your word you're going to be seen as unreliable. Maybe even untrustworthy. People won't want to deal with you, work with your teams, or do business with you at all. Trust is built over time and lost in a moment.

Worst of all, when you don't keep your word, *you* will start to think the same thing about yourself; your mind will tell you that you are unreliable and untrustworthy. That's not good for self-esteem and confidence.

If you don't do what you say you're going to do, you are sending a clear message that your word means nothing. If you want to live a full life, your word needs to become law. What you say is going to happen must happen.

What makes you think you can handle executive level decisions for your firm or handle multimillion-dollar business transactions if you can't email someone back or review a document for someone when you said you would?

Seriously, it's so simple. All you have to do is do what you say you're going to do. And if you aren't going to, then don't say you are!

INTEGRITY IS EVERYTHING

There is something incredibly empowering about doing what you say you're going to do; about following through on your word. No matter how big or small, it feels terrific. Not only because those around you learn to trust your word, but because you believe in yourself and respect yourself. This is a critical foundation for success in all areas of your life.

I have come to know that how you do *anything* is how you do *everything*. You are not what you say you will do; you are what you actually do! This principle or behavior translates into delivering on the significant things in life as well as the seemingly small. Consistently keeping your word is the foundation of integrity.

Honor your commitments with integrity. If you don't, it starts to erode your credibility, builds distrust and limits opportunities.

Those who know me personally know that I commit to a lot less these days. But if I say I'm going to do something, however big or small, I will do it; whatever it takes. I would rather die than go back on my word.

Just ask my wife. Frequently, she will ask me to remind her to do something, and I won't agree to it until I make a note of it or set an alert on my phone. I will not give my word and risk not honoring the commitment.

Let's say you work as part of a high-performing team and you always do what you say you will do. The people around you will build up trust in you and, perhaps more importantly, they will naturally have belief in what you say. Then, when it comes to you sticking your neck out and making a call on something that is hard to predict or may have unfavorable results if you're wrong, the team will rally behind you and support you – because they believe you; because you have established a track record of actually doing what you say you will do.

CONFIDENCE AND SELF-WORTH

Keeping your word builds confidence and self-worth. As you practice keeping your word, you are practicing the process of creation – no matter how big or small. You and your brain will start to get the message that what you say *actually comes true*. This provides evidence to support that you are trustworthy and reliable.

You can tackle bigger and bigger challenges and build more and more confidence. This leads to a more fulfilled life and a feeling of freedom because you start to believe in your own skills and abilities; you begin to believe in yourself and you stop feeling trapped.

Feeling free by keeping your word? That sounds good to me!

FUNDAMENTALS

- Integrity essentially means whole and complete. In other words, doing what you say you are going to do and finishing what you start, consistently.

- All you have to do is do what you say you are going to do. And if you aren't actually going to do something then don't say you're going to do it!

- There is something incredibly empowering about keeping and following through on your word. No matter how big or small the promise, it feels terrific.

- Keeping your word builds confidence and self-worth. You and your brain will start to get the message that what you say *actually comes true.*

EXERCISES

1. Do what you say

Committing to your word is about forming the habit of doing what you say you're going to do.

The trick is to start small and follow through with it. In other words, make it easy to keep your word, don't make it hard. Start small and build integrity.

At first, make it really easy to keep your word (no matter what area of life you're focused on). That way, you show progress, gain momentum, and get reliability on your side. Momentum is significant when creating what you want in your life. Because once you get going in a direction, it is more likely you will continue in that direction.

In this exercise, I want you to identify and write down three things you are going to do – then do them!

I'm not talking about anything significant, I'm talking about simple, straightforward things. Unless you're already a master in this area, you will be surprised how good it feels to do something when you say you're going to do it.

For me, it's like I put a rocket of intention out there and I feel so empowered once I've done what I said I was going to do – no matter how small. It's even better if it involves someone else, perhaps doing something for him or her.

A few work-related examples could include:

> *I am going to cross off three items from my to-do list today.*
> *I am going to send the client an update email at 5pm every day this week.*
> *I will be home by 6pm on Friday night after work for dinner, no matter what.*
> *I will schedule a catch-up meeting for the team at 9am on Monday morning, and book a conference room.*

Summary instructions

1. Read the examples of simple, straightforward things someone may commit to doing.

2. Write a list of **three** things you are going to do. Then do them!

3. Notice the feeling you create when you do something you said you were going to do.

TOOL #6: MEDITATION

———•———

*"If you don't have time to meditate for an hour every day,
you should meditate for two hours."*

– Zen Proverb

TOOL #6: MEDITATION

> med · i · ta · tion
>
> *noun*
>
> 1. the action or practice of meditating.
>
> 2. a written or spoken discourse expressing considered thoughts on a subject.

I recall a serious conversation I had with my boss that would have generated immeasurable stress and anxiety had it not been for my meditation practice.

I had just stepped out of a meeting I'd led. The objective was to come to a consensus on a technical matter. The conference comprised senior individuals from the technical department, as well as individuals from the methodology group.

The good news is that we were all in agreement with the proposed path forward. The bad news is that I mentioned a particular paper that I should not have.

Let's just say that the conversation with my boss after the meeting was heated, and I was the one in the hot seat!

My abilities were called into question. It was challenged whether I could be relied upon to operate solo in the future. There was a risk that specific individuals would lose face. The whole bit. It wasn't good.

What happened next was nothing short of bizarre to me. It was like an out of body experience. I zoomed out and listened to the conversation between the two of us as if I was a third party. I was able to simultaneously hear, understand, and weigh both points of view. I was calm, collected and measured in my response.

I respected the potential severity of the situation and effortlessly came up with an elegant solution to resolve the issue. I didn't take it personally and that was huge for me. Once upon a time, that conversation would have resulted in me feeling sick to my stomach with worry, visibly shaking with anxiety and apologizing profusely.

Instead, I was some kind of emotional ninja. I was able to access the most creative parts of my brain, even under siege. It was quite a remarkable experience.

I was told that meditation helps you to access creative problem-solving ideas, even in a high-demand situation. No shit! This was incredible! Not only was the "bad" experience not bad, I came up with the goods when it was needed.

I was only a few months into meditation and already showing that I was calm under pressure, measured in my responses, and more creative than ever before.

I realized that day, that meditation was now a non-negotiable part of my daily life.

THE STRESS RESPONSE

Job interviews, client presentations and looming deadlines can all be frightening and what most people call "stressful." I would argue that these situations aren't inherently stressful. They are indeed "high demand" but not stressful in themselves. Stress isn't an interview, a presentation, or a deadline. Stress isn't what happens around or to you, stress is your response to a situation.

Stressful situations do not exist. Our programmed response causes stress. In other words, it's our perception that causes anxiety. We experience stress when the perceived demands on us are higher than the resources we believe we have at our disposal.

For example, imagine approaching the end of your workday and getting ready to leave the office. It has been a busy and intense day. You must go by a particular time because you promised your spouse you would be home for dinner. Then the worst thing happens, you get called into the boss's office. There's an error in the final version of the report that is due by the end of the day. Now you need to stay until it's been resolved.

You experience an immediate stress response. You simply don't have sufficient time to get it done and still meet your commitments – a classic example of what can trigger the feeling of anxiety and worry in any of us. What's worse is that our own expectations and projections increase our stress. I guarantee in this situation none of us immediately thinks, "Oh, this will be fine, it'll only take a few minutes to correct the error" or, "It's okay if I'm late home for dinner, my spouse will totally understand." Our expectations and projections about the situation are infinitely worse – especially off the back of a busy and intense day at the office.

That "stressful" feeling comes from the flood of chemicals (specifically cortisol and adrenaline) that get released in the body when the brain launches into speculation. If only we could keep that under control, imagine how much more effective we could be.

STRESS MAKES YOU STUPID

When you perceive a threat – in the example above, a risk to your personal and/or professional reputation – you activate the adrenal system. You trigger the fight-or-flight response.

Thousands of years ago, that was appropriate because we were often faced with potentially life-threatening situations. If you're being chased by a saber-toothed tiger, how much of your body's energy and resources do you want to make available? 100% to run away from the tiger!

Now, though, it's your spouse, or it's your boss, or it's the mortgage payment due in a week. But your system reacts in the same way it would in a life-threatening situation. You're still releasing cortisol, adrenaline, noradrenaline, and all the other stress chemicals into your system.

If you're stressed like this all the time, you are mobilizing resources from your body, including your gut, your elimination system, your immune system, and from your higher brain centers, and you are putting that energy into your muscles to fight or run for your life. That means your memory is weak, your concentration is impaired, you can't digest your food correctly, you can't properly eliminate toxins from your body, and your immune system is compromised. Chronically. All the time.

Stress hormones actually inhibit the immune system. How effectively, you might ask? When doctors want to perform an organ transplant, the recipient is given stress hormones. Why? Because the stress hormones inhibit the immune system so that it doesn't reject the foreign organ.

Unfortunately, in today's world, stressors are 24/7, 365 days a year. You need only turn on the news to see something upsetting and/or terrifying. Whether it's the DOW JONES plunging to an all-time low and wiping out pension fund valuations, a severe and deadly virus scare, or a terrorist attack somewhere in a major city, it never lets up.

The result is a highly stressed-out society. And you are likely one of them.

PROLONGED STRESS IS THE PROBLEM

Historically, our immediate stress response has been pretty useful. 10,000 years later in the modern, corporate world, controlled levels of stress can be powerful motivators in times of laziness or complacency.

Stress is not necessarily a bad thing in and of itself. Prolonged stress is what can kill you.

Unfortunately, we often expect high stress in the workplace, so we accept it and don't do much about it. People I have met or worked with often think that stress gives them their edge – as if stress is the thing that keeps them driven and ahead of the next person. But stress makes you stupid. If you're comparing your performance to the next stressed-out human, then you will never know your full potential.

I stumbled upon an article about researchers wondering what would happen if they set up rabbits to live on grassy areas between the lanes of a freeway in Los Angeles. The rabbits would be relatively safe with fences, but they would be exposed to the constant sounds and fumes of passing cars and trucks.

It turned out the experiment was a disaster for the rabbits. Living on the freeway did all sorts of things to their brains and nervous systems. They failed to thrive and their baby bunnies died. This study drives home the obvious: it's hard to thrive in modern fumes and noise. High stress like this is a given in many organizations. Some days I'm sure some of you feel like these rabbits – you're never off duty, and the pressure to get it all done never stops.

Remember, stress is biochemical. The daily pressures and demands placed upon you in your office, and the number and variety of stressors that come your way (in and out of your work life) do not determine your stress level. Your body's internal response dictates everything. The good news is that the stress response is highly modifiable.

So, we must do something to manage our stress levels. That's where meditation comes in.

WHAT IS MEDIATION?

Meditation has been around for thousands of years. It is a stress-relieving tool, plain and simple – the best one I know. Meditation reduces the amount of stress in the body and helps you to perform better in every area of your life. Meditation is not weird. It's not "out of this world". It's not only for spiritually enlightened monks who live in caves; it's for people like you and me.

Just as your brain has a conscious upper part and a subconscious lower part, your brain also has two halves called hemispheres. You may have heard it said that some people are right-brained while others are left-brained. That's not just a saying, a Caltech Professor won the Nobel Prize in medicine for discovering it. In brief, the left hemisphere reasons sequentially and analyzes details (the analytical mind) and the right hemisphere thinks across categories, recognizes themes, and synthesizes the "big picture" (the creative mind).

Within a minute of starting meditation, your brain and body flood with dopamine and serotonin, which are bliss chemicals. Both parts of the autonomic nervous system, the sympathetic and parasympathetic nervous systems, work involuntarily. Sympathetic is responsible for the response commonly referred to as fight or flight, while parasympathetic is referred to as rest and repair. Meditation essentially shuts down the fight-or-flight response – the fear response – and it stimulates the parasympathetic, or relaxing nervous system of the body.

Meditation helps you to access both parts of the brain simultaneously, which means that, even in a high demand situation, you have access to creative problem-solving ideas.

There's a whole field of neuroscience emerging around the topic of how meditation increases the size of the brain's corpus callosum – the part of the brain which bridges between the left and right hemispheres.

TYPES OF MEDITATION

There are many kinds of mediation. Some forms involve self-reflection, where you sit quietly and ask yourself, "Who am I?" Some styles are called self-questioning – where you question your beliefs. There is another form, which, these days, is called mindfulness – where you practice awareness of your thoughts. In this case the awareness of thought is not thought itself. Then, there is transcendence – using an internal sound to compete with your thoughts to take you to a place where you are left with only awareness.

As we practice meditation techniques, the common objective is getting in touch with our core being; our consciousness. In spiritual traditions, this is called our "spirit."

When you are in meditation, your pituitary gland does fantastic things. It releases oxytocin, dopamine, relaxants, serotonin, and endorphins – basically, everything good that your body can make. These chemicals are released when you make this spiritual connection.

This internal process really is like flipping on a light switch – we can turn on these "juices" of life, just by taking a moment to connect with our spirit. You feel calm and relaxed, your breathing shallows and slows, you feel connected, and you feel unshakable peace. The best part is that meditation doesn't cost anything.

BENEFITS OF MEDITATION

Early scientific studies suggest meditation can produce a long list of tantalizing health benefits. Not least of which, meditation can be the antidote to the voice in your head.

Establishing a daily meditation practice had a profound impact on me. The deep rest that you give your body during meditation is what induces healing and stress release. Less stress in your body is the thing that helps you perform better. I now enjoy feeling fulfilled and I perform at much higher levels than before.

From my experience, there are two main benefits.

The first is focus. With our modern information blitzkrieg, we are more distracted than ever and meditation can help to boost your mental muscle of attention.

The second is becoming an emotional ninja. In other words, no longer being yanked around by your thoughts, impulses, urges and emotions. You become able to respond wisely to things rather than react to them. Responding instead of reacting is a game-changer.

What meditation is doing – especially for beginners – is creating self-awareness. It's waking you up to a fact that most of us are ignorant of, which is that we live with this cacophony in our heads. We're having a non-stop conversation with ourselves that includes random thoughts, urges and impulses. Most of it is negative or desirous, all of it self-referential.

When you're unaware of this, it owns you. You're just acting out your thoughts. Your thoughts become little dictators. An idea emerges, like eating a whole bar of chocolate, and then you do it. Or maybe you think of a statement that's going to get you in trouble, then you blurt it out.

Meditation wakes you up to this mind chatter so that you aren't owned by it.

MISCONCEPTIONS ABOUT MEDITATION

I was skeptical about meditation at first, as I thought you needed to be genuinely enlightened to meditate or you had to be a Tibetan monk living in a cave of nothingness. Then I went through a nervous breakdown, which sucked enormously, but brought me to meditation – the tool that has had the most profound impact on my life.

Many people believe they are unable to meditate because they can't "clear their mind." I am here to tell you that clearing your mind is not possible. Your brain thinks involuntarily, just like your heart beats involuntarily. Try giving your heart a command to stop beating;

it doesn't work. This is why most people think they can't meditate, because they read online or heard someone say that you have to "clear your mind" which is simply not possible.

Nobody cares how many or how few thoughts you have while you're sitting there with your eyes closed in the lotus position. Everyone cares how creative are you, how good are you at problem-solving, and how present you are when you're with them.

I developed a daily meditation practice, and it has improved my quality of life immeasurably. I am no longer stressed. I am calm under pressure. I need less sleep and I have more energy. My creative side comes out even when I'm faced with challenges. I'm more decisive and my actions prove more effective. Meditation enables me to respond wisely rather than react blindly.

The ultimate gift of meditation is liberating you from an attachment to things you cannot control. The liberated no longer needlessly follow urges or cling to experiences. Instead, the enlightened maintain a calm mind and sense of inner peace. Most of all, I enjoy an underlying sense of comfort as I approach everything I do. To me, that's the definition of bliss: knowing that, no matter what, everything will be A-OK. Bliss is not joy or happiness or pleasure. Bliss is a calm, quiet contentedness. Let me tell you, it's a beautiful feeling.

PROCESS OF MEDITATION

You take a bath or a shower when you wake up in the morning because you don't want to bring yesterday's dirt with you into the day, right? If you immediately go to your computer when you wake up, scan through social media, check emails, switch on the news, you take in all the stress of the world. You might cleanse your body by taking a shower, but your mind is still carrying so much stress. Meditating in the morning is just like taking a shower for your mind – it's purifying your mind and purifying your consciousness.

The process is simple: you sit comfortably, relax, and focus your attention on your breath. As soon as you try to do this, your mind will likely go nuts. You're probably going to start thinking about all the things you need to do, what you're going to have for lunch, what time you're going to be able to leave the office, how you're going to respond to that email from your boss. Whatever it is, it's no big deal. As soon as you observe your mind wandering, you may think you have failed. But it's actually a win. Because you are seeing a thunderously undeniable fact that many of us overlook – we have minds and we are always thinking.

Simply repeat the process by bringing your attention back to your breath. If you get distracted still, that is totally fine. Every time you start over, it's like a bicep curl for your brain. You don't have to reach some kind of unique state. Getting "lost" and coming back over and over again is the point.

I couldn't possibly teach you everything I know about meditation in a single chapter of a book, so I recommend you go out and find a meditation teacher who resonates with you. You can do this through in-person training or find one of the many fantastic online courses.

Your teacher does not have to be me, although it would be my privilege to teach you. If you want more information about the training courses I offer, visit Shaping Reality online at:

https://www.shapingreality.com/courses

We will work through a simple meditation in the exercise at the end of this chapter. I can't wait for you to try it!

FUNDAMENTALS

- Stressful situations do not exist – high-demand situations do. We experience stress when the perceived demands on us are higher than the resources we believe we have at our disposal.

The "stressful" feeing comes when the brain launches into speculation.

- Meditation is a stress-relieving tool, plain and simple.

- Meditation reduces the amount of stress in the body and helps you to perform better in every area of your life.

- Meditation helps you access both parts of your brain simultaneously, which means that, even in a high-demand situation, you have access to certain problem-solving ideas.

- Through creating self-awareness, meditation is waking us up to the fact that we have this cacophony in our heads. When you are unaware of this, it owns you.

- Many people believe they are unable to meditate because they can't "clear their mind," but clearing your mind is not possible because your brain thinks involuntarily.

- The ultimate gift of meditation is liberating you from an attachment to things you cannot control, maintaining a calm mind and sense of inner peace.

EXERCISES

1. Introduction to meditation

This exercise is the ideal introduction to meditation.

First, find a safe, comfortable space to meditate. It could be your favorite chair, the sofa, or even your office with the door closed. It's important to avoid interruptions so you might want to warn those around you that you are taking some "me time" and you are not to be disturbed.

Then sit comfortably, with your back supported and your head free. I don't want you standing up, and I don't want you lying down.

Now, close your eyes. I find it most relaxing if the room is relatively dark. You could wear a comfortable eye mask if you wish.

Make no effort to influence your breath; simply breathe naturally.

Focus your attention on your breath and on how your body moves as you breathe in and out. Observe your chest, shoulders, rib cage, and stomach. Just focus your attention on your breathing without influencing its speed or depth.

This exercise is about being present and noticing thoughts as they occur. Meditation is about being an independent observer of your thoughts. So, when your mind wanders – and it will – that's totally okay. Gently return your focus back to your breathing. Then, when you notice your thoughts again, that's fine. Notice that you are observing your thoughts and bring yourself right back to your breathing again.

Maintain this meditation cycle for at least two minutes to begin with. Then try it for more extended periods.

When you initially try this, it will feel uncomfortable. This is not the way the brain was designed to operate – it's a system that is supposed to be constantly looking for problems to help you survive. Getting your mind to slow down and observe your thoughts can be challenging.

Commit to trying this every day for at least seven days. Over the course of a week, you will become increasingly more comfortable with the process. It's particularly interesting to compare and contrast how you feel before and after your meditation practice. Make a note of this and keep track of your progress each time you meditate.

Summary instructions

1. Find a safe, comfortable space to meditate.

2. Sit comfortably, with your back supported and your head free.

3. Close your eyes.

4. Make no effort to influence your breath; breathe naturally.

5. Focus your attention on your breathing and on how your body moves with each inhalation and exhalation.

6. When your mind wanders, gently return your focus back to your breath.

7. Maintain this meditation cycle for at least two minutes to begin with. Then try it for more extended periods.

8. Make a note of how you feel before and after meditation. Keep track of your progress each time you meditate.

Book bonuses

I want you to get the most from your mediation practice so I recorded a guided meditation for you which is available for download.

Visit **www.shapingreality.com/book-bonuses** and download it for free.

TOOL #7: UTILIZATION

---◆---

"A ship is safe in harbor, but that's not what ships are for."

– William G.T. Shedd

TOOL #7: UTILIZATION

u · ti · li · za · tion

noun

the action of making practical and effective use of something.

To understand the importance of the utilization tool I am going to tell you a story.

This ancient talent story tells of a master and his three servants. One day, the master gathered together his servants and informed them he was taking a long journey and would be away for quite some time.

Before he was to leave, he enlisted their service to take hold of his talents. (A talent was a measure of gold coin.). The master addressed his servants and commanded, "Take these talents and make use of them while I am away."

To the first servant he handed five talents, to the second he gave two talents, and to the third he handed one talent. He said again to his servants, "Take these talents, put them to good use while I am away, and report back what you achieved upon my return." The servants were in agreement, and the master went on his way.

The master returned from his trip and, as promised, called everyone together. He asked his servants, "What happened with the talents I gave you?"

He looked to the first servant and asked, "You had five talents, how did it go?" The first servant reported that he took the five talents and put them to work. He recalled that he had some difficulty at first, and then things really worked out well. He proudly reported that the talents grew from five to seven, then to eight, then to nine, and finally to ten. The servant said, "I doubled the talents you gave me from five to ten." The master praised his servant for a remarkable job well done.

He looked to the second servant and asked, "I gave you two talents, what happened?" The second servant reported that the same thing happened to him. He put the talents to work, it was challenging at first, but things really started to work out, and the talents grew from two to three, and then to four. The servant said, "I doubled the talents you gave me from two to four." The master responded, "Congratulations, well done. I am so pleased."

Finally, he looked to the third servant and enquired, "I gave you one talent, tell me what happened." The servant replied, "I took the talent that you gave me, I carefully wrapped it up, I dug a hole, I buried it, and I camouflaged it so that nobody would steal it." He continued, "Fortunately, nobody got it. I dug it up and here it is, safely wrapped. While you were travelling, I did not lose the talent you gave me."

According to the ancient story, the master said, "Take his talent away and give it to the servant who has ten."

What?!

You may be thinking, that doesn't seem fair, the poor guy only has one talent and the other guy already has ten.

The moral of the story is: *What you don't use, you lose.*

Think of it this way: if you tie your arm to your body and leave it there for long enough, you'll never use it again. The only way to retain use of your arm is to continue using your arm.

The same thing that goes for everything else: your mental capability and all human virtues.

Ambition unused, declines. Strong feelings unused, diminish. Faith unused, decreases. Vitality unused, reduces. Energy unused, decreases.

You know the expression, "I'm going to save up my energy?" It's nonsense, you can't do that. It's like trying to save today and put it on the end of the year. It can't be done! If you fail to use it today, then it's lost.

Make sure you are using your talents, abilities, ingenuity, vitality, energy, faith, and courage – every day.

USE IT OR LOSE IT

Picture a battleship docked in the harbor. Every surface is nicked or scratched in some way – it's covered in battle scars and war wounds. The engine is filthy dirty and worn in. The ship is tired and well used. But the ship is far from finished – it's just taking a quick break before getting straight back out there. Because that's what battleships are for; they are built to be out at sea, in harm's way. They are incredibly sturdy and robust; they are made to be used.

Now, think about you achieving whatever it is you want to accomplish in your life. You must put your talents and abilities to work every day in the direction of what you want to achieve. Do not neglect to do the things you can do. Neglect is the key word here. It is a significant reason for people not having as much as they want in their lives: more health, more money, more power, more influence, more everything. They have neglected to do the things they can in order to get it.

Neglect starts off small and grows into more and more. One neglect leads to another. If you neglect to do wise things with your money, you'll probably neglect to do smart things with your time. If you neglect to do wise things with your time, you'll possibly neglect to do wise things with your career.

It can be straightforward making use of the talents you possess. What if *using all you have* was as simple as walking around the block every day for good health? What if *using all you have* was as simple as reading something every day that inspires you to keep your mind thinking and developing? What if *using all you have* was as simple as saving some of what you earn to invest in your financial freedom? What if *using all you have* was as simple as carving out some time every day to spend with your loved ones to connect and deepen your relationships? What if *using all you have* was as simple as adding more value at work to open the door to bigger and better opportunities?

Wouldn't you do all of these things if you knew it to be true?

What better way to show gratitude for all the incredible talents and abilities you have at your disposal than to celebrate them by using them every day? Success in any and all areas of your life has the potential to come pouring in, just as soon as you understand that it's down to you. It's on you to make sure that you use all you have every day. No one can do that for you. Use it or lose it.

USE IT AND MAKE MORE OF IT

There's another interesting angle to this: You know how you won't get more of what you want unless you're grateful for what you already have? Well, I believe that you also won't get more of what you want unless you make use of what you already have and manage what you already have.

This is true for any and all aspects of your life. If you want an abundance of money in your life, then manage the money you have. If you wish for more profound and more meaningful relationships, tend to the relationships you already have. If you want to have more exposure to senior leadership in your career, then give time and energy to the relationships you have at work. If you want a better, higher paying role in your organization, then work hard in your current position and do an outstanding job.

I want to illustrate this point with a short story I love.

STORY TIME AGAIN

One scoop or three?

Picture this, you're a loving parent and you take your little one to the local store for an ice cream cone. It's a real treat for them. Quality time with you, the excitement of choosing which flavor, and tasty ice cream!

You're in the store and your child chooses the flavor they want after much deliberation and a few well-received, complimentary samples.

This magnificent ice cream cone comes over the top of the counter and your sweet child takes it with gratitude and delight with big wide-open eyes. It's just the right size; a large, single scoop of delicious hand-made ice cream.

As you're walking out the store together, your little one is distracted trying to keep the ice cream from melting and running down the side of the cone.

Suddenly, oh no! Your child trips in the doorway, stumbles forward and the ice cream flops to the floor outside. Disaster!

"WAAAAAA!" There are serious tears. The delicious ice cream cone is no more. So sad.

Your precious child looks up at you with those puppy-dog eyes and you agree to go back inside and get a new ice cream cone.

On the way back into the store, they look up and see an advertisement on the wall that they didn't see upon entering the first time.

It's a poster of the new triple scoop giant ice cream cone. Your child's eyes grow to the size of their face, and they turn to you with that longing look once again. Now they want this one. What do you do?

You have a couple of options. You can say no and run the risk of being thought of as a mean parent. Or you can say yes and get them what they want.

Think about it for a minute. What would you do? Seriously.

Most of you will likely come up with the same answer as me and many others, and that is to say no to the triple scoop but follow through with your promise of a single replacement scoop.

I want you to focus on the reason for that conclusion.

Here's the lesson: what makes you think you can handle a triple scoop when you can't even manage a single scoop?

When you show me that you can handle a single scoop, I'll get you a double scoop. Then when you've shown me you can manage a double scoop, I'll get you a triple scoop. And so on.

I believe it's precisely the same way in life. Life wants nothing more than for you to have an abundance of everything you desire. But what makes you think you can handle more of anything when you can't even manage what you have now?

Manage what you have and more will come to you.

———•———

The obvious example here is money. What do you think would happen if the average person came into an overnight fortune? That's right, they'd blow it all. What do you think would happen if a highly sophisticated investor had a massive windfall and woke up one morning to an enormous injection of cash? That's right, they would put their money to work for them and grow their wealth safely and securely.

Show me you can handle what you have and I'll give you more. Don't you just love the idea of that?

Put your talents to use and they will grow. Manage what you have and it will grow. Use it and make more of it! What's not to love about that?

FOCUS ON YOUR STRENGTHS

There's one more angle I want to cover concerning using all you have. It relates to the biggest lie we've been told in life and in business: that we have to work on our weaknesses; we must focus on what we're not good at and make it better.

Well, if you focus only on your weaknesses, you will experience nothing but frustration and inadequacy. Because what you focus on expands.

This phenomenon applies to every aspect of your life. You should clearly put your attention to whatever it is you want to grow in your life: your strengths!

The most successful people in any field have kept their focus on their strengths and not their weaknesses. Think about some of the greats in life and in business: Andrew Carnegie, Bill Gates, Steve Jobs, Richard Branson, Walt Disney, Henry Ford, Albert Einstein and Oprah Winfrey. Do you think they were all without weaknesses? Of course not! They all had flaws, but they definitely didn't achieve their high levels of success by focusing on them. They played to their strengths.

Most of us have the tendency to complain and grumble about something at which we are weak. But have you ever thought of how life would be if you focused solely on your strengths and the positive abilities you possess?

That makes so much more sense to me. Why spend what precious time you have trying to improve the things you're not good at, rather than spending it turning the things you're good at into things you're great at? Perhaps there's a reason you're naturally good at certain things. So, focus on those and do more with them!

We love to analyze our failures. I failed because of that person, that reason, that situation, that mistake, and so on… People aren't satisfied until they have an explanation or someone/something to blame for failure. The result is nothing but a waste of time, energy and effort.

Now, think the other way around. We have all tasted success in some form in our lives. What if we spent time analyzing what we did well and what led to our success(es)? Shifting your focus from weaknesses to strengths instills confidence and positivity in you. It can inspire you to do more of what you're good at and achieve more in the long run.

Knowing what makes you unique and focusing on it will differentiate you from others. This will help you feel more satisfied and, ultimately, achieve more of whatever you want.

FUNDAMENTALS

- What you don't use, you lose.

- Do not neglect the things you can do – put your talents and abilities to work every day in the direction of what you want in life.

- It can be straightforward making use of what you possess:

  - Walking around the block every day for good health;

  - Reading something every day that inspires you to keep your mind thinking and developing;

  - Saving some of what you earn to invest in your financial future;

  - Carving out some time every day with your loves ones to connect and deepen your relationships; or

  - Adding more value at work to open the door to bigger and better opportunities.

- Put your talents to use and they will grow.

- Manage what you have and it will grow.

- Knowing what makes you unique and focusing on your strengths will differentiate you from others. This will help you feel more satisfied and, ultimately, achieve more of whatever you want.

EXERCISES

1. Putting your talents to use

I believe that we all have a unique set of skills and abilities. I also think that it is our mission in life to deliver these skills and abilities to others. (That's a conversation for another time!)

Think about all the things at which you are capable. It doesn't matter how simple or silly any of them may seem. If you are good at something, write it down.

I want you to make a list of at least ten things at which you are capable.

Some people find this difficult because they feel like they are boasting in some way, but no one has to read your list, this is just for you.

I'll give you my list to help you get started.

>*I am good at reading people and knowing what's wrong.*
>*I am good at getting people to open up and share.*
>*I am good at fixing things (I am good with my hands).*
>*I am an excellent public speaker and storyteller.*
>*I am good at explaining complicated concepts in a simple manner.*
>*I am physically strong.*
>*I am good at visualizing in three dimensions (spatial awareness).*
>*I am good at creating a vision and inspiring others to follow it.*
>*I am good at articulating my point, verbally and on paper.*
>*I am good at managing differing points of view (diplomacy).*

Once you have your list, highlight your favorite or most significant three and think about ways you can do more of them every day. Then do them!

Summary instructions

1. Read the list of examples.

2. Write a list of at least **ten** things at which you are capable. Highlight your favorite or most significant **three**.

3. Think about ways you can do more of what you are good at every day. Then do them!

TOOL #8: BECOMING

———•———

"Success is not to be pursued; it is to be attracted by the person you become."

– Jim Rohn

TOOL #8: BECOMING

———◆———

> be· com· ing
>
> *noun*
>
> 1. any process of change.
>
> 2. change involving the realization of potentialities, as a movement from the lower level of potentiality to the higher level of actuality.

Have you ever thought about the process of going to sleep at night? It's an interesting example of attracting what you want by becoming what you must to make it happen.

Think about it: you're at home, watching TV or reading a book, then you decide it's time to go to sleep. That decision kicks off a routine specifically designed to prepare you for sleep. You get a glass of water for the nightstand, you walk upstairs to the bathroom, you brush and floss your teeth, you go to your bedroom, you get changed into your pajamas, you get into your bed, you turn off the lights, you cover yourself with a warm blanket, and you rest your head on the pillow. You lie there thinking about sleep. You are still, warm and comfortable, just waiting for sleep to come. And, of course, it does.

The whole process of getting ready for and drifting off to sleep is an example of manifesting what you want, in this case, sleep. You prepare for it, you expect it and you allow it. Guess what? It comes.

Why can't we apply this principle to anything we want to experience and/or achieve in our lives?

Let's say you want a particular role at work. Why not place yourself in that role in your mind, up front? Surely if you execute the promise and commitment of that role, you will have it? I think it comes down to your mindset. If your mindset is one where you see yourself successful from the start, then the path to what you want is more apparent, the journey to get there is more enjoyable, and the result will match your desire.

So, why don't we do this?

SURRENDER TO WHO YOU NEED TO BECOME

Most people come to believe in life that you do certain things to have what you want so that, someday, maybe you'll be someone.

For example, you do well in school and get an excellent job so you can have a home, a car and so on, to eventually be a respected member of your family and/or community.

This approach of **Do > Have > Be** is a really effective strategy. That is if you want to spend your life struggling!

The do-have-be method puts many people on the wrong path in life. It's a false promise, conditioned into us from a young age without understanding its flaws.

The elements are exactly right, but they are in the wrong order.

If you want to succeed, then don't give any thought to the things you don't have. Instead, focus on being the person you want to become and *doing the things that that person would do.*

Success, happiness, achievement – whatever it is you want – and all that comes with it, will follow.

This reorders the elements to **Be > Do > Have** so that you focus first on who you want to become, not what you want to have.

Generally, we focus only on the way things are and we live "as is." If you concentrate on what is, then you will create and experience more of what is.

If you want to change, then focus on the way you want things to be and live "as if." Think about it, if you're going to live a different life then you need to become a different person.

Whether you're new in your role, in the thick of your career development, or an executive on the front lines of corporate America, there are two methods available to you when planning your journey forward. You can fight your way to the top, as many folks have done, or you can place yourself at the top. Simply be who you want to be.

Neither of these methods precludes you from executing the work (the "do"). The difference is your mindset and the thoughts you allow yourself to entertain.

If your mindset is one in which you wholeheartedly believe you belong (the "be"), and you are capable of fulfilling the "do" then, without a doubt, you will accomplish your goal and you will have what you want to have.

You don't become an entrepreneur by having a successful company. You decide that you want to be an entrepreneur, you behave like an entrepreneur, you do the things an entrepreneur would do, and the successful company follows.

Similarly, you don't become an actress by having a successful acting career. You decide that you want to be an actress, you behave like an actress, you do the things an actress would do, and the successful acting career follows.

You have to "be" and "do" before you can "have."

People around you will always point out "reality" to you. They might say, "Face the facts. Look at what is." Yet, if you can see only what is, then you will create and experience only more of what is. You really do attract what you want. You must be able to put your thoughts beyond what is to draw something different or something more.

The first question is not what you have to do to make a change in your life. The first question is, who do you need to become to create that change?

Become who you want to be – even if it feels like pretending – and the world will adjust.

THE POWER OF INTENTION

It is amazing what happens when you set an intention or make a firm commitment that something is going to be a certain way. Even without knowing "how" you enroll your neurophysiology in finding a way to get you there; just like a heat-seeking missile.

Most people are unwilling to put themselves in the position to commit to a decision – even decisions that are congruent with what they want to create in their life – without knowing the "how." Most people think we are supposed to somehow know how to do something before committing to a decision. Unfortunately, they have this backward. Actually, by making the decision, the "how" begins to unfold.

There was a Harvard brain study done in 2009 where they brought in piano players to play the piano. They studied their brains as they played. Then they studied their brains as they imagined playing the piano and the same parts of the brain lit up. Your brain doesn't always know the difference between imagination and reality.

What happens when you set an intention is that you start to envisage what it looks like. For example, if you stop believing that money is hard to make, you will begin to imagine that making money is easy. As you start to imagine that making money is easy, you establish new neurosynaptic connections in your brain that represent the memory of something that hasn't happened yet. That brain change is what changes the way you think. You start to have ideas and thoughts which are the "how."

Remember the Reticular Activating System discussed in the Gratitude chapter? There is so much information that goes on in our world at all times, we cannot possibly process it all. Our brain filters this information down to a narrow band of what we experience. That narrow band is based on your intentions and way of being.

When you set an intention that you're going to do something or make something happen, you start to imagine it. This shapes the way we think and the ideas we have. You begin to build new neurosynaptic connections as if the future you are visualizing has already happened.

Your brain is a goal-seeking device and this gives you access to the thoughts and ideas necessary to make it happen. This is the science behind why visualization is so important.

VISUALIZE YOUR FUTURE

Visualizing a goal or intention is a powerful way to gain clarity on how to get there and stay on track. If you can picture the outcome in your mind, then you are more likely to go through the process needed to get there. Numerous successful and influential people have talked about the importance of visualization in reaching their goals. If you can dream it, you can achieve it.

Many people dismiss visualization because it seems weird, so let's talk about the logic behind it. Visualizing your goal inspires you to define precisely what you want – not just what you want, but when you want it, who will be there along the way, where your goal will take you, and the benefits of achieving your goal.

Visualization also supports your belief that the desired outcome is possible for you. When you set out to achieve something, there will inevitably be bumps in the road. Visualization enables you to have faith in the process and to keep going after you're faced with a setback.

The best part is, you can reap the benefits of visualization with just a little time and effort.

DON'T FORGET TO TAKE ACTION

One part of the process of creation is arguably the most important and often forgotten: the "do." Too many people are skipping this part of the process and jumping from "be" to "have." The result is a society with an entitlement attitude.

You must take action to produce any results.

Perhaps you set an intention to lose weight and get in shape. Suddenly you notice a new, inexpensive gym has opened up on your route to the office. Don't forget to sign up!

Perhaps you set an intention to broaden your experience at work and make yourself more rounded. Unexpectedly, you overhear a conversation in the breakout area at the office talking about a new and exciting project that needs volunteers. Don't forget to offer your time!

FUNDAMENTALS

- Surrender to who you need to become.

- If you want to succeed, don't give any thought to the things you don't have. Instead focus on being the person you want to become and doing the things that person would do. Success, happiness, achievement – whatever it is you want – will follow.

- If you're going to live a different life, then you need to become a different person.

- If you want to change, then focus on the way you want things to be and live "as if.".

- The first question isn't what do you have to do to make a change in your life; the first question is who do you need to become to create that change?

- It is amazing what happens when you set an intention or make a firm commitment. You enroll your neurophysiology in finding ways to get you there. Your brain is a goal-seeking device, and this gives you access to the thoughts and ideas necessary to make it happen.

- Visualization supports your belief in a desired outcome and enables you to have faith in the process.

- Don't forget to take action!

EXERCISES

1. Who you are now

I believe that making a positive and lasting change in your life requires you to be clear on what you want and, more importantly, who you need to be to have what you want.

The purpose of this exercise is to examine the details of your current identity and then move into your real identity.

The way I want you to achieve this is to answer a series of questions. I want you to be in the right frame of mind to tackle this. I want you to go deep into your heart and soul to answer these questions honestly and without a filter. No one will see what you write down, just like no one knows what you think. This is about you; it's personal.

Here goes:

- What are the details of your current identity? (Are you a parent, a pet owner, a business owner, an artist, an academic, etc.?)

- How might the details of your current identity limit you?

- What do you want in life? (paint the picture of your perfect life).

- Who do you need to become to have what you want?

The details of your identity can work for you or against you, and it's your job to know the difference.

Take the output of this exercise and really think about it. Think about who you are right now and how that translates into what you have in your life. Think about what you want in your life and the person you need to be to have those things.

I want you to come up with at least three actions that you can take now to move forward. They don't have to be significant actions. They don't have to be immediately life changing. I just want you to start thinking and acting like the person you need to be.

For example, maybe you're a budding entrepreneur, and you have all these great ideas, but you feel stuck in your job. You could go online and read about countless people who escaped the 9-5 grind and became successful entrepreneurs and business owners. Read their stories and take note of how they think, approached their transformation, and created what they did in their lives.

Change requires that you surrender to who you need to become. So go and learn about the person you need to be to get what you want. As soon as you become who you want to be, the world will adjust.

Summary instructions

1. Get yourself into a relaxed and open-minded state and read through the questions.

2. Write down your responses to the questions. Go deep into your heart and mind to answer these questions honestly and without a filter.

3. Take the output of this exercise and really think about it.

4. Come up with at least **three** actions that you can take to move forward.

2. Visualize your goals

Dedicate time every day to visualizing your goals. I recommend sticking with no more than three goals. Flying around in your head and jumping between goals and ambitions to imagine your dream life is fun, but it's more powerful to intensely focus on a small number of meaningful goals that will really make you thrive.

Visualize each one for at least a minute; the more detail the better: how things look and feel, what's happening around you, who's there with you, are you smiling or laughing?

It helps to get in the right state of mind before doing this. You can use the same technique of focusing on your breath we talked about in the Meditation chapter. Or, you could even add this exercise to the end of your meditation practice. That's what I do.

Be calm, confident and enjoy the process. You don't get what you want by begging and pleading for it like you're weak; you get what you want by seeing, commanding and celebrating what you want.

Try this for at least seven days. See how you feel about your goals. See what things have come up to help you in the direction of one or more of your goals.

Summary instructions

1. Dedicate time every day to visualizing your goals. Stick with no more than **three** goals.

2. Visualize each one for at least a minute – the more detail the better.

3. Get yourself in the right state of mind before doing this. Focus on your breath or add visualization to the end of your meditation practice.

4. Be calm, confident and enjoy the process.

5. Try this for at least **seven** days.

Book bonuses

As a special treat, I recorded a guided visualization for you which is available for download.

Visit **www.shapingreality.com/book-bonuses** and download it for free.

TOOL #9: RESPONSIBILITY

———•———

"The moment you take responsibility for everything in your life is the moment you can change anything in your life."

– Hal Elrod

TOOL #9: RESPONSIBILITY

---•---

re · spon · si · bil · i · ty

noun

the state or fact of having the duty to deal with something or of having control over someone.

When someone asks you how you're doing, how often do you immediately respond with something negative like, "Oh boy, it's been a rough week" or, "I was late to work this morning because some idiot caused an accident on the highway." Be honest. Do you do that?

Why do we all regularly default to such a response? It seems like a natural reaction for most of us. Many of us don't even realize we're doing it; it's as if we're just programmed to focus on the negative and share our sob stories. Sometimes it seems like people are hard-wired to spew negativity automatically.

I'll tell you why this is – it's because we get sympathy. "Poor you, that sucks", "I'm so sorry to hear that", "It must be hard for you." We do it for the immediate attention and approval. It doesn't matter who you are or how successful you may be, at times we all want attention, support and approval. It's a damn sight more straightforward to get sympathy from those around us than it is to fix the damn problem!

Some people spend so much time feeling sorry for themselves, it's actually disturbing when you notice it. They won't take responsibility or actually do anything to change their circumstances. Instead, they play the victim and soak up all the sympathy they can from those around them.

Tell me, is there anyone you can think of in your life who's always whining and complaining? Always talking about the terrible things that happen to them? Continually telling you about how nothing ever goes their way? Repeatedly saying that someone or something has screwed them over?

Well, let me tell you something: crybabies, whiners and victims don't do well at attracting or creating the life they want. Anyone who suffers from victim thinking and likes to blame others will never experience real success or fulfillment.

TAKE RESPONSIBILITY FOR EVERYTHING

You must own it, all of it: the good, the bad and everything in between. To do anything else is to play the role of a victim and hand over responsibility for your life to someone or something, else. That certainly does not sound like a productive strategy to me. None of this is down to capability – it's down to the fact that you can't do anything positive or be impactful when you're busy making excuses.

Remember we talked about how life isn't happening to you, it's responding to you? Creating success and fulfillment in your life is no different. Success doesn't happen to you; success happens because of you, and the actions you choose to take. When you play the victim, you are turning over responsibility for the events and circumstances in your life. Successful people accept high levels of accountability, and they don't play the blame game – they know that it's better to make something happen than is it to have something happen to them.

Anyone who uses blame as the reason why something did or did not occur will continue to feel miserable.

To take control of your life and tap into your potential, adopt the belief that everything going on in your life – good or bad – is due to something you did. Do you really think that bad things happen by chance? Do you really believe that bad things happen to particular people because they're "unlucky"? Do you really believe that the world is out to get you or someone else in particular? No. Bad things happen because the "victim" gives up responsibility to someone or something else and they think that unwanted results are merely bad luck or misfortune. When in actual fact, it's down to them, and blaming someone or something else only perpetuates the myth that they are a helpless victim.

Decide to take responsibility for all of it. After all, it's your life, so you're in the best position to do something about it, whatever it is. Once you decide to take responsibility for everything in your life, you will find that you are in control and infinitely more likely to come up with viable solutions – no matter the issue.

FAULT VS. RESPONSIBILITY

Many of us are stuck on the difference between fault and responsibility. We've all been stuck in the mode of focusing on something being somebody's fault and blaming them for it.

The thing is, it really doesn't matter whose fault it is that something went wrong or something got broken when it's your responsibility to fix it.

It's not somebody's fault that their father was an abusive alcoholic, but it's undoubtedly their responsibility to figure out how they're going to deal with those terrible and unjust experiences and build a fulfilling life for themselves.

It's not somebody's fault that their intimate partner was unfaithful and broke their heart, but it's undoubtedly their responsibility to take that pain, work through it, and find a way to be joyful in life.

Fault and responsibility don't go together. It may be a hard pill to swallow, but they don't.

When something is somebody's fault, we want them to suffer, we want them punished, we want them to pay for it, and we want it to be their responsibility to fix it. That's just not how it works, especially when it comes to your life and happiness.

All the time you're pointing the finger at someone and focusing on whose fault something is, you are stuck in "victim mode" and therefore suffering.

The road to power is in taking responsibility: your life and your happiness are your responsibility and your responsibility alone.

VICTIM MENTALITY

Good things generally do not happen to people who play the victim, bad things do. All you have to do is ask them. We all know someone who continuously plays the victim. Anyone who plays the victim will happily tell you all about it.

You'll notice the following:

- Bad things always happen to them.
- They are frequently caught up in bad situations and events.
- They are never, ever to blame, someone or something else inevitably is.

Pretend for a second that someone spills a glass of wine in your lap. Maybe you're in a nice restaurant and the friendly server knocks your wine glass over when they're refilling your iced water. It's clearly not your fault, and definitely not something you wanted to happen, but the last thing you want to do is assume the role of a victim. "Ah man, what you do that for? You wasted my nice glass of wine, and now I'll have to get these pants dry-cleaned!" Look at what happens to you when you assume the role of a victim. Doesn't it sound awful?

Would you like that attitude to be part of your job title?

Devan R. Bailey

Founder, CEO, & Part-time Victim

Yuk! No way!

Apportioning blame will never change what happened. Whining and crying won't turn back time. Never claim the position of a victim, especially after you've made the decision to live a life filled with purpose and positive meaning. Do you see the conflict? Instead, take responsibility for the situation and figure out a way to avoid this inconvenience happening again. Especially when the friendly server didn't mean for it to happen. It's not like he or she woke up that morning and decided to seek you out and ruin your evening!

It's easy to blame someone or something else because it takes the responsibility away from you. Frankly, it's much easier to play the victim than it is to step up and take responsibility for the events and circumstances in your life no matter what. Which one feels more empowering to you?

How you address this is to stop thinking that things just happened to you, and to start realizing that things happened because of something you did or did not do.

As soon as you tackle every situation as a person taking action – rather than a person being acted upon – you have more power over the events in your life.

YOU ARE RESPONSIBLE, AFTER ALL

A lot of people subscribe to the belief that you draw or attract things into your life – people, events, and circumstances. A lot of people also believe that we haven't even scratched the surface of understanding the intricacies and capabilities of the human brain. So, is there not the slightest possibility that you had something to do with each of the unwanted things that happened to you? Is it not possible that, on some level, you are responsible for the adverse outcomes that you experience in your life? Whatever happened to you, there was a multitude of inputs that had to align for you to experience whatever you experienced, and you were the only one who experienced that precise event. Had you placed your wine down in a slightly different spot on the table, you could have avoided the lap full of wine. Had you not ordered wine in the first place or sat at a different seat at the table, it would have been impossible for the server to knock over your wine in the precise way that they did.

When you keep getting smacked in the mouth, and it's not getting better over time, maybe you should consider that things don't just happen because of bad luck or misfortune and that perhaps you have something to do with what's happening, or it wouldn't have involved you. Look at it this way: there is only one thing common to all the so-called "bad" things that have occurred in your life: *you!*

You have been blessed with a desire for more (otherwise you wouldn't be reading this book) and you are (hopefully) aware that there is no shortage of success and happiness to go around. So, increase your level of responsibility, assume control for everything that happens in your life, and always remember that nothing happens *to* you, it happens *because of* you!

Bottom line: if you continue down the path of self-pity for the rest of your life, looking for sympathy from anyone who will give it to you, you will live out the rest of your days experiencing different levels of misery.

FUNDAMENTALS

- You must own it, all of it: the good, the bad, and everything in-between. To do anything else is to play the role of a victim and hand over responsibility for your life.

- Decide to take responsibility for all of it – after all, it's your life, so you're the best person to do something about it, whatever *it* is.

- Apportioning blame will never change what happened. Whining and crying won't turn back time.

- It's easy to blame someone or something else because it takes the responsibility away from you. But fault and responsibility don't go together.

- The road to power is in taking responsibility: your life and your happiness are your responsibility and yours alone.

EXERCISES

1. I did this

Everything you do is based on the choices you make. It's not your parents, your past relationships, your job, the economy, the weather, an argument, or your age that is responsible. You, and only you, are accountable for every decision and choice you make.

Indeed, successful people are at the far end of the personal responsibility spectrum; everything happens as a result of their taking responsibility for it, not some external force. This belief allows you to look for ways to improve a situation, move past an issue, and take control of not having bad things "happen" to you in the future.

Here's an excellent habit to form: every time something terrible happens to you or a situation goes the other way to what you wanted, ask yourself, "What can I do to make sure that doesn't happen again?"

No matter what happens, you'll find numerous ways you could have prevented it once you think about it in these terms.

I want you to think of some examples in your life. Make a list of five bad things that have happened.

Maybe you were involved in a fender-bender, which was clearly someone else's fault. Perhaps you were rushing to an important meeting, and someone opened a door into you, which emptied your mug full of coffee all down your shirt. Maybe you missed the last train home because of work, and you had to pay for a cab all the way home.

It could be almost anything. The point is: these are events which you did not appreciate happening and you quickly and easily looked for someone or something else to blame.

Now think about each of these events and come up with one thing you could have done to avoid the adverse outcome.

For the fender-bender, maybe you could leave the house earlier next time when there are fewer cars on the road.

For the spilled coffee, perhaps you use a coffee cup with a lid when carrying a drink between meetings.

For the missed train, maybe you could look up the train times ahead of time and set multiple alarms for when you have to leave.

There are numerous ways each and every situation can be avoided.

The key is, don't blame anyone or anything for your situation or problems. When you do that, you are saying that you are powerless over your own life, which is crap. Reclaim your life by taking responsibility.

Only when you say, "I did this" do you have the power to change it. Your life on the other side – your life of freedom and power – begins when you take responsibility for it.

Summary instructions

1. Make a list of at least **five** bad things that have happened to you. Specifically, bad things that you did not appreciate happening and you quickly and easily looked for someone or something else to blame.

2. Think about each of these events and come up with **one** thing that *you* could have done to avoid the adverse outcome. Remember, there are numerous ways each and every situation can be avoided.

TOOL #10: RESOLUTION

———•———

"For every minute you are angry, you lose 60 seconds of happiness."

– Ralph Waldo Emerson

TOOL #10: RESOLUTION

---

res · o · lu · tion

noun

1. a firm decision to do or not to do something.

2. the quality of being determined or resolute.

One day at school, a kindergarten teacher announces to her class that they are going to do an exercise altogether.

She explains that they are going to go around the room and, one by one, tell the class what they want to be when they grow up.

There are lots of excited faces as well as a few serious faces. These kids are seriously considering how to answer this vital question.

The teacher goes around the room, and there are a whole host of responses. Many you would expect: doctors and nurses, lawyers and accountants, farmers, astronauts, you name it.

One little girl says she wants to vet because she loves dogs.

One little boy says he's going to be a banker, just like his dad.

Then the teacher turns to a one little boy who is looking quite serious.

She asks him, "What do you want to be when you grow up."

He seems to take the question very seriously, and he's thinking about it a lot. Then, all of a sudden, his face and body relax, and he cracks a smile.

He proudly looks up at the teacher and says,

"Ma'am, when I grow up, I want to be happy."

The teacher looks at him and says,

"Oh honey, that's sweet. But I don't think you get the point of the exercise. You're supposed to tell us all what job you want to do when you grow up."

He looks right back at her and says,

"No, ma'am, I don't think you get the point of life."

———◆———

Is it really that simple; to merely make it your intention to be happy? Well, yes. You simply choose to be happy. Happiness is really the point. It's why we're here. The only freedom is internal.

Happiness is an advantage. Happy people live longer, have better relationships, do more, deliver more in their work, and live more fulfilled lives.

People think that happiness is outside of their control and dependent on something or someone else. If the only way you're going to be happy is by having people treat you how you want, and doing the things you want, then you're never going to be happy. Because that's not the way it works.

If our happiness is dependent on someone or something else, then we've completely missed the point. If we allow our mood and behavior to be governed by the reaction of another, then we continue the same pattern. If our happiness is determined by the events and circumstances around us, then we don't stand a chance. We will continue to push against what is and complain about what is not.

Happiness starts with you. Not with your relationships, not with your job, not with your money, not with your circumstances, but with you. Happiness is a choice. Arguably the most important and significant choice you are afforded each and every day. That seems like an idea worth exploring.

THOUGHTS MAKE YOU FEEL BAD, NOT SITUATIONS

Whatever your current situation, if you're feeling bad, it's not because of your current situation. Two people going through the exact same difficulty can have two completely different responses. One may be anxious and stressed, while the other may be peaceful and joyful, no matter how unpleasant things may be.

How we feel about anything in our lives has nothing to do with the events and circumstances of our lives, or what has or has not happened. Our life experience is determined by the meaning we give the events and circumstances that occur in our lives, not the events and circumstances themselves.

This means the external situation isn't causing you distress; your thoughts about the situation are causing you distress. If you want to shift how you're feeling, then change your predominant thoughts. It's really that simple. Does that sound easier said than done? Like anything else, it takes practice. Be aware of your thoughts and observe them when you're not feeling good. You'll be shocked when you notice the things you tell yourself in your head. They're not happy thoughts. If they were pleasant thoughts, then you wouldn't be feeling bad!

It's up to you how you interpret the current situation. Once you notice the negative thoughts, choose to shift away from them, and interpret the situation differently.

When you find yourself in a challenging situation, reach for a good-feeling thought. The most obvious one for me is an appreciation for someone or something in your life. It doesn't necessarily have to be the same subject as the situation in which you find yourself. Shifting to better thoughts means you will experience an immediate shift in how you feel.

Look at it this way: resisting whatever is going on in your life, fighting it in your mind and thinking it shouldn't be this way is not going to help you. Focusing on what you don't want and thinking about how wrong something is will not change your circumstances and certainly won't make you feel good. You have a much better shot at making the best of a bad situation if you can approach it from a positive angle or a place of appreciation.

THE MIND UNDIRECTED

The distress we experience when something harmful or unwanted happens can be attributed to our undirected mind looking for problems. The brain isn't designed to make us happy and fulfilled, it's designed to make us survive. We operate, if undirected, in survival mode, constantly identifying and magnifying potential threats. Your mind makes everything a matter of life and death, even though we're not being attacked by saber-toothed tigers anymore. Most of our undirected thoughts are fear-based. If we leave our ancient survival software in charge, there is little chance of enjoying life. The mind is excellent when used as a tool, it's not so great when it's calling the shots. If you allow your two-million-year-old brain to run your life instead of you, the result will be a life filled with stress and anxiety.

We often assume that bad feelings are just an inevitable part of life, and we live this way because it's the path of least resistance. There is another path. One that starts with consciously directing your thoughts so that *you* are in control of how you feel.

When you feel love, joy, gratitude, compassion, creativity, or any of the empowering emotions, you are feeling good. When you feel good, you seem to know exactly what to do, and you generally do the right thing. That's because you are at ease, your heart is alive, and the best of you comes out. Nothing feels like a chore and everything flows effortlessly. You experience very little fear or frustration. You're in alignment with your core. Have you ever felt like this?

When you feel anger, fear, worry, resentment, or any of the disempowering emotions, you are hurting on the inside. Everyone experiences distress in their own way. The specifics don't really matter because they all feel bad.

CREATIONS OF THE MIND

Most people make unconscious choices based on habit and conditioning, so are at the mercy of their own minds. Most of us haven't trained our minds, we've let our environment do that. What's shocking is that it doesn't matter if the problem is real or not; whatever we focus on, we feel, regardless of what actually happened.

Recall an event that upset you. Perhaps a time when you felt frustrated, angry, worried, or even overwhelmed. Can you see how this was caused by your perception of the situation?

For example, have you ever experienced thinking that a friend did something mean to you, or said something horrible behind your back? It really doesn't feel good. You dwell on it, you replay it in your mind, you imagine the worst-case scenario, and think through all the possible consequences. You quickly become hurt and angry. How could your friend treat you this way? Then you discover you were mistaken and your friend did nothing wrong at all. All is forgiven! Back to normal, like nothing ever happened. What was the point of all that distress?

You created it in your mind. The reality didn't matter. Your focus created negative feelings and your negative emotions created your negative experience. It was all based on perception and listening to the fear-based thoughts thrown out by your undirected mind.

Once you're aware of this, you can change and free yourself from this nasty habit. It all starts with the realization that you have a choice.

You can continue to believe in the false illusion that you can't do anything to resolve or improve a situation, or you can remember that you alone have the power to determine what something means.

We think that what is wrong is outside of us and therefore out of our control. But what is wrong is within you and very much within your control. Taking control is not difficult once you understand what is going on.

Our job is to create happiness for us, and the only way to do that is to choose not to feel bad. Shift your thoughts, and you will shift how you feel and what you experience.

I appreciate this is contrary to popular belief. So often we see someone on our way to work or in the office looking down in the dumps. When we ask them, "What's wrong? Why are you looking sad?" we generally get a response like, "Oh nothing, just Tuesdays suck!" Of course, we respond with empathy and compassion, saying, "I hear you; it'll be Friday soon."

Now imagine you see a friend or colleague with a huge smile on their face, looking overjoyed. You ask them, "Hey, what happened? Why are you so happy?" They respond, "Oh, no reason, I'm just feeling great!" You might think they were crazy, or you might think there was something seriously wrong with them.

Why is it that we need a reason to feel good, but we don't need a reason to feel bad?

HAPPINESS IS A CHOICE NOT A CONSEQUENCE

Our lives are shaped by our choices. If you look back over the last ten years of your experience, I'm sure you can remember several important decisions that have changed the course of your life. Maybe your choice about where to go to school, what jobs to apply for after college, or who you chose to move in with. Can you see how different your life would be if you had made different choices?

We tend to burden ourselves with all kinds of choices in life – about our careers, where to live, who to go out with, and whether to believe in a higher power. In the end, you need only make one fundamental choice: do you want to be happy or not? Once you make that choice, your life becomes clear.

Happiness doesn't come as a result of people, events and circumstances in our lives. Happiness is you making the solid choice to think good-feeling thoughts and focusing on appreciation for what you have. Choose how you feel and peace can be yours immediately.

Most people don't make a choice to be happy because they believe that happiness is not within their control. Someone might say, "Of course I want to be happy, but I didn't get that promotion at work." That person wants to be happy, but only if their conditions are met. That wasn't quite the question. The question was whether you want to be happy. If you keep it simple, you will see that it is really under your control. The common problem is that your rigid set of conditions get in the way.

There is no question whether happiness is under your control – of course, it is. We just don't really mean it when we say we want to be happy, because we want to qualify it. We want to say that we will be happy as long as certain things do or don't happen; as long as our preferences are met. This is why happiness appears to be a consequence of events and circumstances outside of our control. It's the conditions that limit your happiness because you simply cannot control everything going on in your life, nor can you keep things precisely the way you want them.

If you want to be happy, then answer, "yes" to the question without conditions. This means that you want to be happy from this point forward, no matter what.

You might not get promoted, you might have a disagreement with one of your colleagues, you might even lose your job due to cost-cutting. Pretty much anything could happen between now and the end of your life. But if you want to be happy, then you have to really mean it when you choose to be happy. No ifs or buts, it must be a *resolution*. It's not enough to say you would *like* to make a change or you would *like* to be happy all the time: you need to *own the choice*.

Remember, the feelings you experience are the result of where you choose to focus your thoughts. You alone are responsible for how you feel and what you experience in life because you have the power to choose your thoughts and direct your focus.

COMMITTING TO UNCONDITIONAL HAPPINESS

The slightest thing happens to you and you give away your happiness. You were having a great morning until someone cut you off on your way to work. It got you worked up and you stayed like that for most of the day. Why? What good came from letting that event ruin your day? There is no rule to say that you have to do that. You really do have a choice. Examine what's happening at the moment and question whether you are willing to give away your happiness. If someone cuts you off, rise above it. Smile and remind yourself that you have no idea what that person is going through. If you really want to, you can.

Surely the purpose of life is to enjoy and learn from all of our experiences. I don't think we were put here to feel bad. You're not helping anyone by being miserable. Regardless of your spiritual beliefs, we were all born, and we are all going to die at some point. During the time in-between, it's your choice whether you want to enjoy the experience. Events and circumstances don't determine your happiness – they're just events and circumstances. You decide whether to be happy.

Look at it this way, you could be happy simply to be alive and breathing. Break the habit of thinking that there's a reason not to be happy. The only logical thing to do is to enjoy life's experiences. Things are going to happen. Why not be happy about it? You don't gain anything by being disturbed by life's events. That does not change the world, it just means that you feel bad. There is always the potential for something to bother you, but only if you let it.

The path to happiness, no matter what, is to give a resolute answer; to cut off other possibilities. You must mean it when you say you are going to be happy no matter what. If you choose that you are going to be happy from this moment on, no matter what, then you will be happy.

Unconditional happiness is the highest state there is. You don't have to do anything weird and spiritual; you don't have to study to become an enlightened monk; you just have to mean it when you say that you choose to be happy no matter what.

MENTAL TRAINING

When you feel like you can't control what's happening, and you can't make a negative into a positive, challenge yourself instead to control the way you respond to what's happening. That's where the power is. External forces outside your control can take away everything from you, except one thing: your freedom to choose how you respond.

Something will inevitably happen to challenge you. Your mind is going to tell you that it's unreasonable to be happy all the time when these things are happening. This is a test of your commitment and this is precisely what stimulates personal growth. It's easy to say you're happy when things are going your way. It's not so easy to say it the moment something unwanted happens.

In these moments, you must choose whether or not to go back on your commitment. Are you willing to go back on your resolution just because an event took place in your life? An infinite number of events could take place that you haven't even thought of. The question is not whether they are going to happen; things *are* going to happen. The issue is whether you are committed to being happy, regardless.

The key is to learn to keep your mind disciplined enough so that it doesn't trick you into thinking that, this time, it's worth giving away your happiness. If you slip, get back up. Pick yourself up, remind yourself of the commitment you made to stay happy no matter what happens. Remind yourself that all you want is to be at peace and to appreciate life. Your happiness is not dependent upon the behavior of others. It's hard enough when your happiness is dependent upon your own actions.

Every time part of you wants to be unhappy, remind yourself of the utmost importance of your commitment. Do something to feel better at that moment. Use incantations, go for a run, listen to loud music, dance around like a hooligan, or appreciate something precious in your life – whatever it takes!

Here's the best part of all: the more you do this, the more you practice shifting your state, the better you get at doing it. Mental training alters brain structure. Just as you increase physical strength by lifting progressively heavier weights, you can systematically train your mind and emotions. The tenacity of spirit and toughness of the body are part of the same continuum. Choosing to pay attention to empowering thoughts and images stimulates new pathways and, repeated continuously, they become stronger. It's like doing another arm curl in the gym every time something comes along and tries to knock you down. You grow stronger and stronger. You gain more and more momentum.

If you are committed, you can enjoy life's experiences, no matter what happens. If you stay happy no matter what, you have succeeded in the best way possible. Make that your ultimate challenge and stay happy no matter what. If you do this, great things will happen for you.

Will you commit to feeling good not only when things go your way, but also when things go against you? I, for one, am done with feeling bad. I choose to live every day to the fullest and find the good in everything, including moments I don't like so much. Don't mistake my words, I'm an imperfect human (just ask my wife!) However, I am accomplished at managing my emotional state and I am continuously improving.

Feeling good all the time, no matter what, is the ultimate freedom. It is the ultimate gift for yourself and for those you love. Life is just too short to not enjoy every moment of it.

FUNDAMENTALS

- The distress we experience in our lives can be attributed to our undirected mind looking for problems. The brain isn't designed to make us happy and fulfilled, it's designed to make us survive.

- Most people make unconscious choices based on habit and conditioning, and are at the mercy of their own minds. Because most of us haven't trained our minds, we've let our environment do that.

- Our job is to create happiness for us, and the only way to do that is to choose not to feel bad. Shift your thoughts and you will shift how you feel and what you experience.

- External forces outside of your control can take away everything from you, except one thing: your freedom to choose how to respond.

- If you are resolved, you can enjoy life's experiences, no matter what happens.

- Feeling good all the time, no matter what, is the ultimate freedom. It is the ultimate gift for yourself and for those you love.

EXERCISES

1. Public resolution

If you're ready to make the commitment to being happy and feeling good, no matter what, I recommend that you write it down and share it with others. There's nothing like making a public resolution and having others hold you accountable.

In this exercise, draft an email explaining your choice and why you have made it. Then, send your email to three people you respect and ask them to tell you, gently, if they ever see you slipping.

By writing down your resolution, you make it real, and you make a firm commitment. You never know, you may even inspire those you send your email to, to follow you in making this commitment themselves.

Below is a template email you can use if you wish. Feel free to make edits as necessary and make it your own. This is the email I sent to those closest to me when I personally made the commitment to being happy no matter what.

To: *[email address]*

Subject: Unconditional happiness resolution

Hi *[their name]*

I have made a resolution to be happy no matter what. I will do everything in my power to live from my heart and find the best in every situation.

I know that the emotional state in which I live is the result of where I choose to focus my thoughts. I alone am responsible for my state of mind and for my experience of this life. Feeling bad is just the result of my undirected mind looking for problems. I don't have to believe these thoughts or identify with them. I either master my mind, or it will master me.

The most critical choice in life is whether or not I want to be happy, no matter what happens to me. I now commit to enjoying life, not only when things go my way, but also when things go against me.

I'm done with feeling bad. I'm going to live every day to the fullest and find something to appreciate in every moment, including the ones I don't like. When I get off track, I will snap myself back immediately, BECAUSE LIFE IS JUST TOO SHORT NOT TO BE HAPPY!

My ask of you: Please tell me (gently) if you ever see me slipping.

Feeling good all the time, no matter what, is the ultimate freedom. It is the ultimate gift for me and for those I love.

Yours,

[your name]

Summary instructions

1. Draft an email explaining your choice to be happy no matter what and why you have made it.

2. Send your email to **three** people you respect and ask them to tell you, gently, if they ever see you slipping.

2. Positive rant

In this exercise, we are going to use the concept of a "rant" to blast out on paper all the things that are great about a situation or person. The idea is to shift your focus quickly from negative to positive on a given topic. This is a tool I use to shift my thoughts and feelings about a particular person or situation when I feel bad and can't immediately shake it.

For example, let's say that you are mad at someone. You know that you are not in a positive state, you know better than to indulge in the negativity, but you just can't shift your mood because you are mad at this person.

Well, here's what you do: grab a piece of paper and a pen, put the name of the person at the top of the page and start writing all the things you like about the person; all the things you are grateful for about this person; all the things you are thankful for that they have done for you.

It will be slow to start – your mind is throwing all kinds of negative thoughts at you, which get in the way and force you only to focus on what you don't like. Do not let these thoughts get in the way. Think of one positive thing, then another, and another. As you do this, they will start to flow much more quickly.

Here are two examples of positive rants I did. They were both related to work and the stress/pressure I was feeling. One about my career as a whole and not being able to shake the feeling that I hated my job. The other is about the "Monday morning feeling," written early on a Monday morning when I really didn't want to get up and get out of the house.

Chosen career

- I am proud to work where I work.

- I am surrounded by incredible people.

- I get support from my friends and colleagues.

- It is a highly intellectual work environment.

- I experience a variety of day-to-day tasks.

- It is a fast growth/developmental environment.

- No day is the same in this job.

- I have many exciting and meaningful problems to solve for clients.

- I can help others – colleagues and clients – every day.

- The financial rewards are excellent.

- I have a clear career progression.

- I have built a strong foundation of knowledge in a broad range of areas.

- I have developed skills/abilities I can take with me into everything I do.

- I have enjoyed so many different experiences.

- I have learned about myself in challenging situations.

- I have developed clear and concise communication.

- I have honed my writing skills.

- I have sharpened my decision-making ability.

- I have grown in confidence.

- It is a pleasant work environment with excellent facilities.

- Great perks!

- I am well looked after.

- I work with genuinely bright and lovely people.

- I enjoy fun and laughter at times.

Monday mornings

- I have the whole week ahead; it's a fresh start which feels good.

- There's less pressure on Mondays than later in the week.

- Everyone is in the same situation, so we lift each other's spirits.

- We have the opportunity to talk about our weekends with one another.

177

- We can plan our next weekend right away and look forward to it.
- The roads are often quieter on a Monday morning.
- The office is a little slower and calmer at the start of the week.
- The day always goes quickly in the office on a Monday.
- I feel terrific after a productive day, then it's time to head home.
- After Monday, we have already made progress in the week.
- I always feel good and energized after the weekend.

I can honestly say that I have found this quick process to be very effective at shifting my focus and resulting feelings about a given situation or event.

Read the list back to yourself. It really lifts your mood by changing your perspective on the situation or event you are focused on so negatively.

Now it's your turn.

Summary instructions

1. Identify a situation or a person that is bothering you. The idea is to shift your focus quickly from negative to positive on a given topic. Grab a piece of paper and a pen and put the name of the person or situation at the top of the page.

2. Start writing all the things you like about this person or situation; all the things you are grateful for about this person or situation; all the things you are thankful for that this person or situation has created for you.

3. Read the list back to yourself and notice the shift in your mood and perspective about the situation or person you were previously focused on so negatively.

PART III:

LIFE ON YOUR TERMS

———◦———

"It is better to live your own destiny imperfectly than to live an imitation of somebody else's life with perfection."

– Anonymous, The Bhagavad Gita

BRINGING IT ALL TOGETHER

————◆————

If I could distill the contents of this book into a simple philosophy, this is how you can escape from emotional prison:

1. *Take command of your mind*

It's all about mindset. From the moment you wake up, to the moment you rest your head at night, everything is up to you. All too often we are derailed by that disempowering voice in our head. When we don't see the mental chatter for what it is – just noise – it controls us.

The voice in our heads is bringing to our attention all that could go wrong. It's a deep-rooted part of our ancient survival mechanism, designed to keep us safe. It is certainly not designed to make us happy. You've learned that this is not you; this is just programming from your experiences playing back. It becomes the way of being for so many because we don't know that disregarding the fear-based thoughts is an option. Dissociating from your thoughts gives you enormous power.

You've learned that your beliefs determine where you end up in life. This is because whatever you believe, at a subconscious level, will dictate your thoughts, moment to moment. How you think determines how you feel, how you feel motivates your actions, and your actions produce the results you experience in your life. So, the results you have in all areas of your life directly correlate to your predominant thoughts – what you believe.

You must become conscious of your unconscious world to make any changes in your external world. There's no other way around it. To go against this is like trying to climb a mountain wearing a concrete backpack. That's what most of us are doing. It's no wonder that life in the corporate world is burning us out. Beliefs are actually choices made over and over again. We may have experienced something when we were young, unconsciously attributed meaning to it, and that led to a belief. Now you are aware of it, you have an incredible gift: the ability to choose how you respond.

The moment you become aware that you have unconsciously decided something that isn't congruent with how you want to experience your life, you have a responsibility to make a different choice.

You've also learned how meditation can help you become an emotional ninja, no longer yanked around by your thoughts, impulses, urges and emotions. Meditation wakes you up to this mind chatter so that you are no longer owned by it. You become able to respond wisely to things rather than react to them, and this is a game-changer.

2. Manage your emotional state

Your emotional state at any point is absolutely critical. If you're down in the dumps, then you're going to think and act differently and get different results compared to when you're pumped up and excited to be alive. Managing your state is all about staying "up" no matter what. Just as there are things you allow to bring you down, there are things that raise you right back up in an instant.

You've learned about the incredible power of gratitude. The best way out of any unwanted emotional situation is gratitude. To experience the enormous impact of appreciation, you must practice it every day and make it a way of life for you. The words *thank you* are so, so important.

You've learned about the power of being present. If anxiety and worry are your favorite flavors of suffering, then focusing on the present moment – the here and now – is your ticket to freedom. Even when your day seems to be spiraling out of control, being present is a way to handle any situation.

The method for being present is relatively simple, but you must practice it. Whatever you are doing, focus entirely on doing that one thing. Pay attention to every aspect of the experience rather than everything else you're telling yourself you should be doing. You will notice your worries melt away, and you'll enjoy every present task much, much more.

You've also learned about present moment awareness: the power in separating what is from your thoughts about what is. It's never what actually happens in your life that makes you feel bad, it's your thoughts about it that makes you feel bad. When something unwanted occurs in your life, and suffering arrives, ask yourself what is truthful about the situation. Separating the truth of the matter from the narrative about the situation will allow your feelings to pass.

3.   Commit to happiness, no matter what

There is remarkable power in choosing your attitude, even under the worst circumstances. Events and circumstances beyond your control could take away everything you possess, except for one thing: the power to choose how you respond. Committing to unconditional happiness will teach you about your mind, your heart, and your will. Choosing to enjoy life, no matter what, is the ultimate gift.

You learned that happiness is a choice, not a consequence. Happiness starts with you, not with anything else going on in your life. The distress you feel when something unwanted happens can be attributed to your undirected mind looking for problems. Your job is to create happiness for yourself, and the only way to do that is to choose not to feel bad. The average person doesn't seem to need a reason to feel bad, so why should you need a reason to feel good?

You also learned that your life and your happiness is your responsibility and your responsibility alone. To take an alternative view is to play the victim, and good things generally do not happen to people who play the victim – bad things do. The road to power is in taking responsibility for everything in your life.

GO YOUR OWN WAY

You can determine the direction of your life, and I think you should. That's what it means to be human. If you look around you, at life in general, we are not doing anything significantly different from other animals. They are born just as we are born. They grow up just as we grow up. They reproduce just as we reproduce. They die just as we die. Nothing is significantly different.

The critical difference is this: we can conduct these simple things in life consciously. That is the significant thing about being human.

Let's say you conduct your hand consciously. Your hand will do what you want, right? Suppose you command your thoughts consciously? Now your thoughts will do what you want. If your thoughts are taking instruction from you, deliberately, you will keep yourself in the highest state of feeling. Your entire life will come with ease.

So many people, in the pursuit of happiness, think they will be happy when everyone and everything is a particular way. If this happens or that happens, then you'll be happy. Those are conditions and it means that the world has to function *your way* for you to be happy. You tell me, is it easier to change all the people around you and all the events that take place in your life, or to take charge of yourself?

I think it's fair to say that, for most of us, the majority of what we want to happen, happens. It's just that we are focused on the few things that did not happen. Let's say you get 90% of what you want, it's the 10% you focus on and complain about. Most of your pain and anguish comes from your preferences not being met, not a lack in your life.

Not all situations will play out the way you want because there is more than just you involved. Everything need not happen your way. But if you choose to be happy no matter what, then you are happy. Suddenly you are no longer in pursuit of happiness, you *are* happy. You are no longer tense about anything, there is no metaphorical gun to your head, and you do everything to the fullest, joyfully, because you don't care what happens. Even if you don't get the result you wanted, you are still happy. It's a beautiful thing.

ONWARDS AND UPWARDS

———◆———

Let me tell you what I have come to know for sure.

You are your own rule maker and you set the guidelines. You decide how well you have done and how well you are doing. You are the only one who can determine who you are and who you want to be.

If you want your life to take off, imagine it the way you want it to be and take steps towards that every day. Hold in your mind your highest vision for yourself. Imagine who you would be if you lived that vision every day. Imagine what you would think, what you would say and do, and how you would respond to others.

When you notice a thought that is incongruent with your highest vision, change to a new thought immediately.

When you say something that is out of alignment with your vision for the future, make every effort not to say something like that again.

When you do a thing that is misaligned with your best intentions, decide to make that the last time.

There's only one thing you can truly control: how you will choose to respond to any given event or circumstance.

Everything in this world was born out of an idea; a thought. Everything started with a thought. So, it follows that you should get that right first.

Taking control of your mind and choosing better thoughts to pay attention to is at the heart of all this. This requires work, and it involves continuous conscious choice-making. This whole process is about self-awareness and a move to consciousness. What you will find out when you start living the life you want is that you've spent most of your life unconscious, unaware of what you are choosing in the way of thoughts, words and actions. You've been on autopilot.

Now you have the tools you need to break free and live a full life. It's up to you. You have the power to create anything and everything you want in your life. It was there all along, just waiting to be tapped into.

I genuinely believe that we are all meant to have a joyful, expansive experience, and how you do that is your call.

Nothing is more important than feeling good, and you have complete control over it because you can choose a thought that makes you feel good or a thought that makes you feel bad. You have the choice in every moment; you are the master of your own destiny; you are the captain of the ship; you are in command and you determine the course of your life.

Don't be afraid to go after what you want. If it turns out great, then you can rest easy, knowing that you went down the right path at that time. If it turns out to be a disaster, well then, you will have learned something you needed to learn that could not have been taught any other way. When you adopt this kind of mentality, there's something positive waiting for you no matter the outcome.

Looking back, perhaps the most significant barrier I faced was the fear of failure. Failure somehow meant to me that it was all over. I now refer to failure as temporary defeat. Because you can't actually fail if you don't give up.

The majority of people see success and failure as some sort of a play-by-play. If you succeed, you succeed, and if you fail, you fail. But maybe there's something much bigger going on. Maybe if you step back from individual successes and failures, and look at the bigger picture, life will feel a whole lot less daunting.

There will be ups and downs for sure. But if you don't at least try to be the best you can be, how will you ever know what's on the other side?

There's actual, real work to do in shaping your life the way you want – your health, your relationships, your career, all of it. Waiting for the "perfect moment" or for the "most convenient time" could very well mean missing opportunities for the rest of your life.

If something is stirring in you now, and you know what it is, do it. There's no need to overthink it. A mistake here and there isn't going to kill you, so don't waste too much time worrying about what will be. Would you rather fail with courage and try again, or sit idly with fear? Only one of those options gives you the chance to live freely.

Do you want your life to be a warning or an example? All great stories are about finding freedom. Think of *Gladiator*: the story of a once-powerful general, sold into slavery to be trained as a gladiator. He rises through the ranks to avenge the murders of his family and his emperor, finding ultimate freedom in his death. How about an extraordinary journey out of pain and darkness into love and light? Or a story of someone in a dead-end job lost and emotionally bankrupt, taking command of their mind, becoming emotionally free, and finding happiness in anything and everything in their life? That could be you.

Greatness comes from the desire to be extraordinary and to do extraordinary things – to reach beyond the status quo and relentlessly pursue the best version of yourself. It all starts with your intentions. When you aim higher, you force yourself to grow.

We all have greatness inside of us. We merely have to choose to be great and with a finite amount of time to live your best life, the time to embrace your inner greatness is always now.

You have everything you need to call the shots and to make things happen for you. You were built for this, so go out there and get to work.

I will leave you with this. There are only two pains: the pain of hard work and the pain of regret. The pain of hard work is measured in ounces, while the pain of regret is measured in tonnes.

You have precisely one life in which to do everything you will ever do. Act accordingly.

WRITE IT DOWN

You must have heard the suggestion that there is power in writing something down. I genuinely believe that is the case.

Personally, I think it drives clearer thinking. I can hold only so many thoughts in my head at once. I find it incredibly helpful to write down my thoughts, facts and feelings. Then I don't have to use my mind for remembering; instead, I can use it to think more clearly.

Having things written down serves as a reminder of what to focus on. It also gives me an overview and makes it easier for me to draw connections and identify new insights.

So, here's what I want you to do. Go back to the contents page and circle the heading of your favorite chapter, or the tool you found to be most impactful. Don't overthink it. One of the chapters or one of the tools stands out to you more than the others. Just pick one.

Okay, picked one? Great. Now quickly write it down below and answer the following questions:

> *What stands out to you about the chapter or tool?*
> *What does it make you think and feel?*
> *What does it stir up inside you?*
> *What is the first action you are going to take in this area?*

Life is a lot like driving at night. You don't need to see the whole route to reach your destination. Your headlights illuminate the next 200 feet in front of you as you move forward.

So, you don't need to know how to get to where you want to be, you just need to decide what you want and take the step that's right in front of you in the direction of what you want.

This is your first step forward.

Over to you.

What are you waiting for?

Get writing!

_____

_____

_____

_____

_____

_____

_____

_____

_____

_____

_____

_____

_____

_____

_____

Acknowledgments

My thanks to:

The strong, loving, and influential people in my life – those who have sacrificed for me, pushed me to be more, and helped me get back up when I fell down. Without you, I would not be who or where I am today. You have helped to shape the empowering and self-serving beliefs I have today. Your love, support, and guidance have shaped my life and, honestly, opened my heart and mind to opportunities and possibilities I once only dreamt of. There's no way to repay you for the wealth of information you have given me, or for the wealth that I have created in my life as a result. Instead, I simply say thank you and make a commitment to give my time and love generously, to share my knowledge to help and to liberate others.

Tim Pettingale, Joseph Alexander and the team from Self-Published. You helped me create something of which I am incredibly proud. Thank you.

Fools, friends and family who helped me during the editing process. 40,000+ words take effort to read, digest and critique. I very much appreciate your time and attention.

More About Shaping Reality

So many of us have grown up in this modern society that thrives on performance, competition and perfection.

Intensified workloads, unreasonable expectations, and difficulty balancing life has led to crippling anxiety, overwhelming worry, and debilitating stress levels.

The truth is, you are far more extraordinary than you were ever made to believe. The constant feeling of stress and pressure is NOT natural. I believe that we were not made to be small or less, we were made to feel fully alive.

This is why I decided to create *Shaping Reality* — a coaching and training organization on a mission to equip you with the knowledge and practices needed to live an extraordinary life.

No matter where you are, or where you want to be, we have the tools and resources to help you be the best version of you.

COURSES – The tools and practices to absolutely crush it in life.

https://www.shapingreality.com/courses

COACHING – Helping you think differently, live consciously and feel truly alive.

https://www.shapingreality.com/coaching

WORKSHOPS – The information needed to lead with positivity and power in these changing times.

https://www.shapingreality.com/workshops

You really do have the power to up-level your life and the lives of those around you.

I'm excited for you to be part of Shaping Reality and I look forward to serving you.

Printed in Poland
by Amazon Fulfillment
Poland Sp. z o.o., Wrocław